THE *Spirit-Filled Family*

Tim & Beverly LAHAYE

HARVEST HOUSE PUBLISHERS
Eugene, Oregon 97402

Scripture quotations in this book are taken from the New King James Version, Copyright © 1979, 1980, 1982 by Thomas Nelson, Inc., Publishers. Used by permission.

Published in association with the literary agency of Alive Communications, Colorado Springs, Colorado.

THE SPIRIT-FILLED FAMILY

Copyright © 1995 by Tim and Beverly LaHaye
Published by Harvest House Publishers
Eugene, Oregon 97402

Library of Congress Cataloging-in-Publication Data

LaHaye, Tim F.
    The Spirit-filled family / Tim and Beverly LaHaye
        p.   cm.
    ISBN 1-56507-332-0
    1. Family—Religious life.   2. Marriage—Religious aspects—
Christianity.   I. LaHaye, Beverly.   II. Title.
BV4526.2.L26   1995   95-8018
248.—dc20   CIP

Printed in the United States of America.

95 96 97 98 99 00 — 10 9 8 7 6 5 4 3 2 1

Contents

*To our children, Linda, Larry, Lee, and Lori,
whose lives have been enriched more than
they realize because in the mercy of God,
their parents were introduced to
the Spirit-filled life when they
were very young.*

Introduction

Bev and I have not always been happily married. For several years in the earlier stages of our marriage our relationship deteriorated so much that we didn't communicate very often, and even then we irritated each other. On a scale of 0 to 100, I would have rated our marriage about 25; Bev says it was more like 30. The only things that held us together were 1) rejection of divorce as a solution, 2) four children, 3) vocational necessity (divorce would have ruined my career—churches take a dim view of employing divorced ministers), 4) phlegmatic stubbornness and choleric determination. Bev was too stubborn to admit defeat, and I was too bullheaded to give up. Does that sound happy? It certainly wasn't!

Strangely enough, we were both very dedicated Christians. Telling it now, I realize it doesn't sound like it, but we really were. We met in a fine Christian college where we were preparing to serve the Lord. Bev dedicated her life to Christ when she was 14, hoping someday to serve as a missionary. At a summer camp, when I was 15, I had surrendered to the call to preach the gospel. Bev finished high school early, so she was only 17 when I met her at the dinner table the fourth week into our freshman year of college. I had done a two-year stretch in the Air Force and was 20 at the time.

We didn't fall in love at first sight, but I was a rather determined young man. So even though she was afraid to show too much interest in me at first, we gradually fell in love. I kept after her and finally convinced her that "it was the Lord's will" that we get married the following July (long before either of us was mature enough). But who can tell two young people in love to "slow down"? My mother couldn't, and neither could Bev's parents.

During our junior year in school, we were called to a little country church in the South Carolina mountains, where we served the Lord for two years, and my parishioners graciously displayed the spirit of long-suffering as they allowed me to practice my first batch of sermons. After graduation I prayed desperately that our two-year growth from an average attendance of 75 to one of 77 was not a true picture of my preaching ability.

As newlyweds enjoying the challenge of our first church, life was exciting and dynamic. Except for financial difficulties, we didn't have many problems those first three years. Linda, our firstborn, came during that time, and we both loved her dearly. Except for a few of Bev's periods of stubborn silence which followed my occasional eruptions of anger, we got along fairly well. I'd score our marriage about 85 for the first few years.

Somehow, in the providence of God, we were miraculously called to pastor the Minnetonka Community Church in a suburb of Minneapolis. A delightful six years ensued (except for the 200,000 tons of snow I was forced to shovel). The church, which was constituted of some of the finest people in the world, grew from 90 in Sunday school to almost 400. I was busy with two lengthy building programs in my first full-time pastorate, and Bev was active as a pastor's wife, junior department superintendent, and young mother of three (our two boys were born during this time). I would score those years about 90 for our ministry and 70 for our marriage.

Our call to the Scott Memorial Baptist Church of San Diego, California, was another act of God's providence. Our daughter Lori was born there, but even then our marriage relationship was going downhill. We kept up a good front and always did the "right thing." Although we experienced many happy times, they were occurring at increasingly detached intervals and were accompanied by a heightened amount of tension. By the time we were 10 to 12 years into marriage, we had become two strong-willed personalities of the opposite sex who lived in the same house, shared the same children, and held the same basic spiritual views and values, but disagreed on almost everything else. As Bev matured, she refused to be bullied into doing unwanted tasks, and the more she balked, the more dominating I became. We won't bore you with the gory details; they were similar to those of millions of other unhappy couples.

The strangest part of all this is that we were both very dedicated Christians and tireless servants of a very fine Bible-believing church. In fact, the church was growing well and people were receiving Christ regularly, forcing us to plunge into two building programs in four years and eventually expand to three Sunday-morning services. The folks seemed to enjoy my expository preaching with its strong emphasis on practical Christian living.

But something was missing. We knew absolutely nothing about the Spirit-controlled life, particularly at home. We could live the Christian life away from home because difficult circumstances came in shorter and less-pressured doses. But at home the pressures became too intense. And when we failed to control ourselves, we compounded the problem. Many folks have the mistaken idea that pressure *makes* someone's spirit. That isn't true; it only *reveals* his or her spirit. Actually, what we are under pressure is what we are! We were deteriorating under family pressure, and so was our marriage.

At a time when our marriage score was hovering between a rating of 25 and 30, Bev received an invitation to attend a Gospel Light Sunday school conference at the beautiful Forest Home conference grounds. That week she had the life-changing experience of being filled with or controlled by the Holy Spirit. She called me on Wednesday and enthusiastically urged me to come up for the last day. Since she had been away from home for four days, our marriage relationship had jumped to a rating of about 35, so I reluctantly accepted. What I didn't realize was that the speakers had addressed her biggest problem the first of the week, but had switched to mine for the last two days. I arrived just in time to hear Dr. Henry Brandt tell the story of my life. Oh, he was referring to another angry choleric minister who had come to him from the Mayo Clinic with bleeding ulcers (I only had pains in my stomach which I refused to take to the doctor), but I recognized the story's applicability. When Dr. Brandt finished, I admitted to myself what an angry, selfish hypocrite I had been. So I slipped out of the chapel, got alone with God, and for the first time in my adult life was filled with the Holy Spirit. I didn't see any visions and I made no audible sounds, but I underwent a life-changing experience with God. Because Bev and I came down from that mountain filled with the Holy Spirit, He changed our marriage, family, and ministry. Gradually our selfishness, my anger, Bev's fears, and our joint bullheadedness have been replaced by the love, joy, and peace which the Holy Spirit provides when we are controlled by Him.

Today we can honestly say that we enjoy the most ideal marriage relationship two people can share on this earth. When in 1968 I wrote *How to Be Happy Though Married*, which God has been pleased to use in helping over 900,000 people (assuming one reader per copy), I dedicated the book to Bev with these words:

> *This book is lovingly dedicated to my wife, Beverly. Her patient understanding and loving tenderness have made our marriage an increasingly joyous experience. Her inner beauty, "the hidden woman of the heart," like her physical beauty, has improved through these twenty years. Every day I thank God for bringing her into my life.*

That statement is even more true today than when first written. Now I would add, "She has become my dearest friend."

We are convinced that the Holy Spirit's filling is the key to happy family living, for that is the context of Ephesians 5. It is certainly the way He worked in our own marriage. However, we have observed that most Christians go to one of two extremes regarding the filling of the Holy Spirit, thus missing the practical purpose for which He has come into their lives. They either concentrate on an emotionally oriented experience that centers on themselves, or they ignore Him altogether. As we shall show in this book, the Bible teaches that the Holy Spirit's filling is really for family living, not for what Christians do at church. In fact, we tell people to examine their conduct at home to see if they are truly filled with the Holy Spirit. For if we can live the Spirit-controlled life at home, we can live it anywhere. Why? Because what we are at home is what we really are!

If your conduct at home during the past two weeks offered little evidence that you were filled or controlled (they mean the same thing) with the Holy Spirit, then you aren't filled with Him, regardless of what the people at church or work think of you. Ask yourself this question: "If the members of my family were secretly polled on whether or not I was filled with the Spirit during the past two weeks, what would they say?" That is the best indication of whether or not you are.

God the Holy Spirit always enriches and beautifies the life He fills. What better gift can He bestow upon a Christian than to make his home the most wonderful place on earth? And that is exactly what He wants to do for all His children. We have lived both ways and thus can testify that Spirit-controlled family living is the only way to live. No doubt that is the reason God has given us a ministry of sharing the principles of Spirit-controlled family living with thousands of people around the world. He says in His Word that we are able to comfort others with the same comfort we ourselves have received from God (2 Corinthians 1:4).

In 1972, when God specifically led me to found Family Life Seminars, I never dreamed where such a decision would lead. At first I conducted Friday evening and all-day Saturday seminars on family living wherever five pastors in a city invited me. Bev stayed with the children at home, where she conducted women's retreats. Then for three years I teamed up with Dr. Henry Brandt and later with Dr. Howard Hendricks. Altogether, we conducted 150 seminars in 68 cities of the United States and Canada. Seven years later our youngest child went off to a Christian college, and Bev was free to travel with me and share in the seminars. Since then we have conducted 900 seminars in 46 countries of the world, and related principles of Spirit-controlled family living to one million people. Our mail from many who have attended the seminars confirms that lives were transformed after being filled with the Holy Spirit and using His power to apply the biblical principles for marriage and the family. As I travel throughout the country, holding Family Life Seminars in some of the nation's leading churches, I meet many couples who have been helped significantly by learning these timeless principles for happy family living.

In 1979, Beverly, together with nine other women, founded Concerned Women for America. Today, CWA is the single largest pro-family women's organization in the nation, and is now located in Washington, D.C. Her activities at Concerned Women for America, where she serves as president, find her working with some of the key conservative leaders in the nation's capital. Just this week she testified before the powerful Ways and Means Committee, where she made a strong appeal for greater tax deductions for families with children.

This book—not a repetition of our other writings—contains the principles that we teach at our seminars. It particularly emphasizes the ministry of the Holy Spirit in the home life of the Christian. Some of the chapters are written by Bev, some by me, and others are shared. Forgive us if we relate personal stories to illustrate biblical principles, but we want you to know that God's plan really works. It has for us, and it will for you. We trust this book will illustrate what God the Holy Spirit has done with our lives, blending us together so that we can accomplish more work as partners than either of us could do separately. It is our prayer that He will do the same for you. We are convinced that the principles in *The Spirit-Filled Family* will enable you to enjoy a good family life as well as raise good children in our present hostile culture.

Chapter 1

The Importance of the Family

The family is the most important single factor in the molding of a human being. It either prepares him to reach for his ultimate destiny and fulfillment, or it cripples and inhibits him from attaining his original potential. When a society disregards its families, it suffers irreparable loss. If it disregards its families long enough, the society passes into oblivion as did many civilizations of the past.

The first institution God founded was the family. In fact, He established only three institutions: the home (or family), government, and the church. These three institutions form the basic building blocks of a sane and well-ordered society.

Family. The family (Genesis 2:18-25) was to provide a haven for its members to prepare them to enter society and serve God and their fellowman.

Government. Human government was founded by God (Genesis 9:4-7; 10:5; Romans 13:1-8) for the purpose of protecting man from depraved individuals who either had not learned or refused to obey God's principles of respect for others and their property, so necessary to civilization.

Church. The church was instituted many centuries later because the family and government had both failed so miserably to protect man from himself and his fellowman. The basic sin of self-will and selfishness in the human heart had brought society to a place where most human beings were slaves of other human beings. Into such a sinful environment God sent His Son, Jesus Christ, to die for man's sin that man might be "born again," gaining a new nature. This would enable him to follow the time-honored principles for achieving the happiness and fulfillment in life which God had revealed in His Word. To communicate these principles, He founded His church. The primary purpose of the church which Jesus Christ promised to build was the teaching of the gospel and the commandments of God (Matthew 28:18-20).

Whenever the church has done her work positively, she has so strengthened her families that they have served as a stabilizing influence in society, producing freedom, liberty, and opportunity unequaled in any of the pagan cultures of the world. When the church has failed in her teaching role, it has been at the expense of both the family and society.

Today the best marriages and families are found in Christian homes where members actively attend churches that teach biblical principles for family living. The young people from such homes are the leadership hope for tomorrow. As the founder and a former president of Christian Heritage College, I was always thrilled to see the sterling young people who came to us from many Christian homes. I am aware of today's general family breakdown that is making serious inroads even into the church, but I am also aware that many Christian homes are stronger and better than they have ever been.

The home and the church are not competitive, but naturally supportive institutions. They must be; otherwise, their children will not survive in today's hostile culture. In fact, if it had not been for the church, humanists of our day with their teachings of "no absolutes" and "do what you feel like doing" would have destroyed our culture. Placing little or no value on the home, humanists, if they had their way, would abolish it and allow government to raise the children. That may be appropriate for mind control, but it is certainly destructive of freedom, happiness, and fulfillment.

Anything that is harmful to the home is the enemy of society, and the secularistic teaching of humanism has become our culture's most destructive family force today. The three most powerful agencies of society are the media, the entertainment industry, and public education. All are controlled by humanists, and all are harmful to the home. Even Bill Clinton, in his 1995 presidential State of the Union address, called on the media and the entertainment industry to "show more restraints in programming in relation to violence and 'inappropriate behavior.'" His statement was met with thunderous applause and a standing ovation from the senators and congressmen present. Maybe, just maybe, America's voting will turn to the right and we will see our nation adopt family-friendly policies that will help the church restore family values in this country in preparation for the twenty-first century.

The Family Is Basic to Adults

The family was God's first institution because it is basic. Man by himself is incomplete. Almost everyone is familiar with the story in Genesis 2 of lonely Adam and his naming of the animals who came before him. The passage concludes with the words: "But for Adam there was not a helper comparable to him." Then we read the beautiful story of God's special provision, for He took from Adam a rib, made the woman, and "brought her to the man" (Genesis 2:20-22). Many theological romanticists suggest that this was the world's first wedding and that God performed the first marriage ceremony. From that day to this, no other factor in human life has been more significant than the home.

In my book *How to Win Over Depression*, I cited the

25-year study of stress on human beings by Dr. Thomas Holmes of the University of Oregon. He listed 43 crises that occur in life, according to their severity in producing stress. Not until two years after the book was published did I notice something extremely significant about his list. The top 50 percent of life's stress-producing problems relate directly to the home. Consider the first ten items listed below:

Rank	Crisis	Points
1	Death of a spouse	100
2	Divorce	73
3	Marital separation	65
4	Jail term	63
5	Death of close family member	63
6	Personal injury or illness	53
7	Marriage	50
8	Job firing	47
9	Marital reconciliation	45
10	Retirement	45

Except for a physical injury (to which he ascribed 53 points), six of the top seven traumas of life have to do with family disruption (assuming that a jail term separates family members). According to Dr. Holmes, family problems are at least twice as stress-producing as others, and in many cases are three or four times as great. Of his 43 common problems in life, I counted 23 that related to the family.

One conclusion we can draw from this crisis chart is that family problems cause us the most stress because the family is the most important factor in our lives. Show me a person who enjoys dynamic family life, and I will show you a basically happy person. In fact, family fulfillment leads to life fulfillment. But without family fulfillment, nothing else in life really matters.

What could possibly cause successful businessmen or great geniuses who receive world renown to spend their final years in despair? Usually it is because they became alienated from their families. And more often than not, they sacrificed family to gain notoriety. That is a price too great for any adult to pay, particularly in terms of a lifetime investment.

The Family Is Basic to Children

A child's family is easily the most important single influence in his life. Nothing else even runs a close second. The home molds character and personality. Inherited temperament makes a significant contribution, to be sure, but the direction which temperament takes is dependent on a person's home life and training. For example, if two choleric infants are born into contrasting families, they will grow up to be entirely different. Both will be active, hard-driving individuals, but the one from a rejecting home, where he watches his father rebel against authority, will more than likely turn out to be a gangster who takes advantage of his fellowman. The lad who grows up in a loving home, where values are communicated and laws are respected, is likely to become a very productive adult who makes a significant contribution to society.

The family histories of Max Jukes and Jonathan Edwards provide a startling illustration of this contrast. Max Jukes, who lived in the state of New York, did not believe in Christian training and married a girl of like character. From this union 1026 descendants have been studied. Three hundred of them died prematurely. One hundred were sent to the penitentiary for an average of 13 years each. One hundred ninety became public prostitutes, and there were 100 drunkards. On today's economic scale, this family cost the state over six million dollars. There is no record that members of this family made any positive contribution to society.

Jonathan Edwards, who resided in the same state, believed in Christian training and married a woman of like mind. From this union 729 descendants have been studied. Three hundred became preachers of the gospel. There were 65 college professors, 13 university presidents, 60 authors of good books, three United States congressmen, and one vice president of the United States. It is impossible to underestimate the contributions this family made to the state of New York and to the country. The Edwards family is a sterling example of the biblical principle: "Train up a child in the way he should go, and when he is old, he will not depart from it" (Proverbs 22:6). In spite of the enormous influence that TV and education exercise over the moral values and character of our children, nothing is more influential than the home and family.

The diagram below indicates that although other important factors shape a child at various stages of life, none of them is more influential than the home. Thus, it is rightfully located in the center of the circle, for the home serves as the core of character-building. This should be reassuring to Christian parents, who wonder if they can raise their children properly in this day of moral collapse. One young couple protested, "We aren't going to have children; things are so socially corrupt that we refuse to bring a child into the world for fear of losing him to the world." We quickly countered that their position reflected complete unbelief in the power of God to use their Christian home to prepare the child for life. Let's face it: Life offered little sweetness and light in the first century either, but Christians married and raised fine families, and they

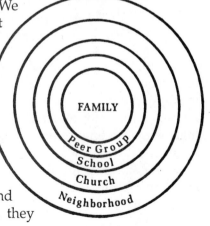

FAMILY

Peer Group

School

Church

Neighborhood

took over the Western world in less than 300 years. Many excellent young people are being produced by active Christian families today. Of course, we possess assets unknown by first-century Christians, such as a vital church influence on both parents and young people.

The Influence of Early Childhood

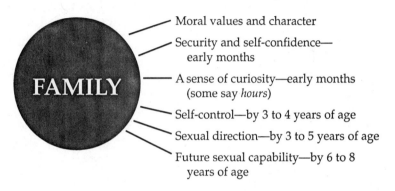

Moral values and character

Security and self-confidence— early months

A sense of curiosity—early months (some say *hours*)

Self-control—by 3 to 4 years of age

Sexual direction—by 3 to 5 years of age

Future sexual capability—by 6 to 8 years of age

The preceding diagram lists some of the profound influences on a child which affect his entire life. Moral values and character are not taught; they are "caught" in the home. A child whose parents demonstrate respect for the rights of others grows up with a healthy attitude toward his fellowman. If he sees his parents lie and cheat, he will do likewise.

The child who is loved intimately from day one will be far more secure (within the framework of his temperament) than if rejected. A study of children taken from their mothers at birth in the hospital and not returned until six hours later for their first feeding showed them far less curious and alert at one month than those placed in the arms of the mother as soon as both were cleaned up. Some doctors have determined that long periods of sterilized separation are emotionally harmful to the newborn. Obviously, God intended the newborn to go right from the mother's warm womb to her warm body. In such areas, modern medicine is seldom an improvement on nature, for researchers have discovered that breast-fed baby boys are far less likely to stutter at five or six years of age than those raised on a bottle. Even the doctors who made the study were not sure whether the distinction was the result of the more powerful mouth muscles developed through breast-feeding, or stronger and better emotional confidence due to love, closeness, and "stroking."

In the counseling room, I have repeatedly encountered the connection of a bad home life with sexual dysfunction. When I counsel a frigid wife, I look first for a rejecting father in her childhood. Show me a little girl of five or six who can run to her daddy, sit on his lap, and kiss him anytime she likes, and in 15 or 20 years I will show you a young woman who is emotionally prepared to be a sexually responsive wife. Show me a little girl whose father rejects her spontaneous expressions of affection, and I will show you a girl with a predisposition toward frigidity before she is six to eight years of age.

The best sex education occurs long before a child's first day of school. Two parents who love each other and demonstrate this affection in the home almost never raise frigid or homosexual children. During research for *The Unhappy Gays*, my book on homosexuality, I discovered why so many people have bought the lie that homosexuals are "born that way." Because the signs appear so early in life, people *think* homosexuality is genetic. Actually, homosexuals' sex direction was predisposed before they were three years of age by a rejecting father and a domineering or smothering mother. The best preventive against homosexuality in either a boy or girl is a wholesome love relationship with the parent of the opposite sex and a positive role model by the parent of the same sex. Masculine fathers who loved and spent time with their sons rarely saw them become homosexuals until recently. (Today there is so much propaganda and encouragement given the practice that many young people experiment with it until it becomes a learned behavior. Under these circumstances, almost anyone can be swept into it. But even then the best preventive is a good home life.) It has long been observed that angry, hostile parents produce angry, hostile young people. Polite, gracious parents similarly reproduce themselves in the lives of their children. Doubtless, that is the reason the teenager who stands out in my mind as the most thoughtful, considerate, and polite youngster I've ever known came from a home where her mother was equally gracious. "A chip off the old block" is more than an expression. It is a truism. And provided the "block" is what it should be, the "chip" will be right.

Marriage Is Basic to the Family

Although a close parent-child relationship is extremely important, it is not the principal basis for a good home. God instituted the family with marriage first and then children. Somehow, today the emphasis has shifted until we have established child-centered homes. This is a mistake. Good marriages are primary to good homes. If you mistakenly sacrifice the marriage for the children, in so doing you will destroy both.

Children understand by nature that they are number two in the hearts of their parents. And if we analyze children's status within the home, we discover that it is transitory at best. Youngsters are destined to spend only five years in intimate dependence on the parents, and then for the next 15 years gradually grow independent of them. By contrast, parents are destined to spend upward of 50 years together and will be joined to each other (under ordinary circumstances) for the rest of their lives. A child, then, almost from his inception, is being readied for graduation. In a home where he is given a number-two love priority, any child will flourish.

The worst emotional basket cases that I have dealt with

among young married people were not those rejected by their parents, but those who had become substitute lovers or—because of their parents' inadequate marital love—had been subjected by a love-starved parent to a "smother" mother/father love. A tragic illustration came to our attention recently. After eight years of marriage and two children, a wife began complaining about long evening telephone calls when her husband would lie across the bed and recount to his mother every detail of the day. Eventually, she went into his room to find that he had moved out, leaving only this note: "I don't want to be married any longer. I am returning to live with my mother. She is still the number-one woman in my life." "Smother" mother-love had done it again, generated by a selfish compulsion to keep her son for herself.

Some years back when Bev and I traveled to five Communist countries of Eastern Europe, we noted a basic similarity. The stronger the Communist party, the less freedom and more drab and disillusioning the lifestyle. But the people had one thing in common. Whether they went five months without meat, as they did in Russia, or whether they had to line up hours in advance on a cold day just to buy a pair of crudely manufactured shoes, there was one special object which even the Communists couldn't take from them: their family. Whether in a drab 20' by 20' unheated apartment or in just a single room, they shared their lives with each other. The Communists know that the most volatile ingredient in causing a revolution in their country would be the senseless breakup of home and family.

One day we saw a beautiful illustration of the importance of the home. The delightful old lady who waited on our table in a Romanian hotel's restaurant had become quite friendly with us in spite of our language barrier. Usually quite somber in her sad and backward surroundings, we saw her eyes light up as a young woman in her early twenties walked up and kissed her warmly. The young lady, turning to us with a most pleasant smile on her face and an arm around the portly woman, proudly announced, "Me mama." That look spoke volumes! As long as you have someone who loves you, someone who cares whether you live or die, life is worth living, even under communism.

Next to God Himself, nothing is more important in your life than your family. Are you giving it that kind of priority?

Chapter 2

The Decline of the Family

"Our civilization is headed for collapse if we don't start caring more for children and strengthening our family life," warned two nationally known experts on human development. Dr. Harold Voth of the famed Menninger Foundation elaborated, "I honestly believe that civilization as we know it is imperiled by the forces that are eroding the family. The American family is deteriorating because of the social and economic stress, and today's child is growing up alienated, frustrated, and bored."

But that isn't all these experts concluded. One predicted a chain reaction that could have devastating results on our culture: "Unless this trend is halted, children growing up today will have trouble forming families of their own and the problem will perpetuate itself." He went on to say that of all the problems facing Americans today—energy shortages, unemployment, pollution, communism—none is more pressing than the crisis in our family life. "Destroy the internal structure of the family and you are going to wreck civilization."

This pessimistic appraisal is not unrelated to the latest divorce statistics. In 1976 we crossed the one-million-divorces mark for the first time. In 1977 we crossed it again and added almost 30,000 more, which increased to 1,130,000 during the mid-eighties and has leveled off, even though by 1995 there were more divorces than marriages each year.

Many experts claim that 51 percent of those who marry today will get a divorce—which, of course, is not good news for the families of the future. It is an accepted fact that children of divorced parents have less-stable marriages than those whose parents stay married for life. In addition, experts warn that for every official divorce there is at least one "poor man's divorce"—that is, when a man will not or cannot afford an attorney, he just runs away from his family and his responsibilities. Sociologists estimate that currently 10 to 11 million children are being raised by one parent due to divorce. It is further predicted that 25 to 30 million will be raised by a single divorced parent for at least part of their first 18 years of life. One bestselling author suggests that the pressures of life have become so intense today because of the rapidity of change that it is wrong to think about remaining married for 50 years. He proposes that the average person divorce and remarry every ten years. That certainly would provide "change," but would it result in improvement?

Of the 46 countries in which we have traveled, no other nation comes even close to approximating the wonderful lifestyle Americans enjoy. It is hard to believe that America's most important institution, the family, is on the brink of extinction. In my lifetime the divorce rate has risen from 27 percent to the latest high of 51 percent. (Among the under-21 age group, it is over 60 percent!) Marital instability has become so prevalent that a group of humanistic psychiatrists at a meeting in Los Angeles concluded that since there is no solution to the constantly increasing divorce rate, they could only suggest that we "abolish marriage."

These social planners (or wreckers—depending on your point of view) forget one important fact: Man didn't think up marriage on his own. Unattached men and women didn't live for centuries in communal groups, then meet in a cave somewhere and decide to initiate the new and exciting concept of marriage. No, it was instituted by God when only one man and one woman were present on the earth. Therefore, marriage is basic to society. Fortunately, the antifamily mood seems to be changing in our country. If trends continue to move in a more conservative or values-oriented direction, we may see a welcome improvement in family stability. Certainly, that will be good news for the 50 million or more children whose present family life will have a powerful influence on their future attitude toward marriage, children, and family.

Signs of Moral Collapse

It is interesting to compare conditions in our country during the mid-nineties with those of Greece and Rome just before their decline. They are tragically similar:

1. Departure from original religious beliefs
2. Obsession with recreation
3. Inflationary spiral which made the purchase of a home prohibitive for the average couple just starting out
4. Widespread sexual infidelity and a sharp rise in homosexuality
5. A constant clamor for democracy
6. Decline in the birth rate so that the population did not replace itself. (The latest report indicates we now have 1.6 children per family —down from 2.4 just ten years ago.)

Have you ever wondered why this once-great nation, built largely on the principles of the Bible, began to imitate the pagan nations that finally destroyed themselves? This course didn't originate with a single choice but with a series of decisions.

Causes for Today's Family Breakdown

We have been in the family-helping business for over 25 years and, for the last 15 in Washington, D.C., we have lobbied Congress and the White House on many antifamily programs and legislation. So, naturally we have given a great deal of attention to what has caused the decline of the family in our nation and the erection of a distinct antifamily culture. We have discovered at least 15 powerful agencies whose policies for the past 50 years have had a detrimental effect on the family. You need to know what they are so you can steer your family away from their influence. They will be given in detail later in this book. Here, however, you should know of a serious change in major institutions that has taken place during the last half of this century. Following are the most harmful forces against the American family.

1. *The entertainment industry and media (which have more influence on our culture, the family, and individuals than does the church).* For the first 350 years of American history, the church had more influence on our people, institutions, and families than almost all other agencies put together. No longer is that true. Now that role is in the hands of Hollywood and Broadway writers, producers, playwrights, actors, and others who seem not to have any moral values and are not responsible to anyone but themselves.

TV and movie film provides the filmmaker with the most powerful vehicle to the human mind in the history of mankind, for it combines the visual and auditory means of access to the human brain at the same time. When that vehicle is used for the spread of the gospel or moral principles for living, it is extremely positive. When it is used as most of it is today, it is very harmful to both society and the family.

As we pointed out in our most recent book, *A Nation Without a Conscience,* it is obvious to anyone who can see that the small number of those who make up the entertainment industry have been busy spreading their antimoral, anti-family values on our nation's 250 million souls, or at least on those who watch the industry's productions. Based in Hollywood and Broadway, filmmakers have rarely represented the American people, and are much more liberal in politics and moral values than the average citizen.

Having been in church work all our lives, we find it painful to admit that the men and women in the entertainment industry have more influence on the conscience of our nation than do preachers, parents, teachers, or anyone else. In fact, it is a very small group of individuals that holds our nation's morals hostage. Less than a few thousand movie-studio owners, producers, television station and network owners, actors, and others control this morally uncontrolled industry whose greatest victims are our nation's children. There is no more powerful tool in the battle for our culture than the entertainment industry, most of whose members have adopted the values of secularism.

This is certainly true of most current movies and TV productions. Most TV sitcoms are not fit for viewing and today's films not only glorify the immoral, but also promote the antimoral.

The problem is compounded when the media turns to these "role models" for advice on the burning issues of the day and gives them a national audience to communicate their antimoral ideas.

Elizabeth Taylor, the eight-times-married movie star of yesteryear, often pops up on national shows to offer her ideas on subjects ranging from AIDS to virtue. As I write these words, her picture of 20 years ago is featured on the front cover of the *Saturday Evening Post*—a magazine that used to be an exponent of family and moral values. Donald Trump, the divorced New York playboy and casino owner, was recently featured with his new wife—a woman he lived with who broke up his first marriage—on the front cover of *Vanity Fair* to offer his views on "family values."

Even before reading the article, you know he doesn't understand the "family values" that you and I revere—traditional moral values that helped make this the greatest country on earth.

Ever since Clark Gable uttered the "d" word for the first time on-screen in *Gone with the Wind*, profanity has gradually eroded decent speech and is the rule rather than the exception today. Most films out of Hollywood today use profanity as though everyone talks that way. Though usually adding nothing to the story line, profanity has come to be expected in movies and is now common on late-night television and increasingly tolerated in prime-time shows.

What else are our children watching on television? Morality in Media tells us:

> By the time the average child graduates from elementary school, she or he will have witnessed at least 8,000 murders and more than 100,000 other assorted acts of violence on television. Depending on the amount of television viewed, some youngsters could see more than 200,000 violent acts before they hit the schools and streets of our nation as teenagers.[1]

Most of us are numbed by violence on television, another group of us is made paranoid, and a third group is actually enthralled by the vile practices on the screen! At a time when the incidence of murder, rape, and even child molestation is increasing, the keepers of the entertainment industry in Hollywood are producing films that many people claim educate viewers about how to perform such vile acts. Producers deny that they are responsible for the acts of violence committed by viewers, but evidence shows that in real life many people do imitate what they see. Throughout America many "copycat" crimes have left victims dead or maimed for life.

While we are discussing powerful influences, we cannot ignore the rock-music industry. The obscene, immoral, and blasphemous lyrics, along with the suggestive and blatant gestures of rock stars, influence many young people to follow those immoral lifestyles. Rock musicians are consistent in their disdain for and irreverent treatment of Jesus Christ. For instance, in *The Advocate* newspaper, Madonna said: "I think they probably got it on, Jesus and Mary Magdalene."[2] Sheer blasphemy!

The music of the forties and fifties was about love, companionship and the heartbreak of love. It certainly was not Christian music, but the songs did not encourage immoral acts or blaspheme Jesus Christ. Today's rock stars have become idols and role models for many of our youth. Teens listen to hours of blasphemous words from heavy-metal rock stars—the more blasphemous the lyrics, the larger are the crosses the stars hang around their necks. In May 1985, Madonna told *Spin* magazine: "Crucifixes are sexy because there's a naked man on them."

The greatest sin of Hollywood is blasphemy. The names of God and His Son, Jesus Christ, are invoked frequently in one form of profanity or another. You will remember that one of the Ten Commandments warns that "the LORD will not hold him guiltless who takes His name in vain" (Exodus 20:7). We have often wondered if some of the stark Hollywood tragedies have had anything to do with the industry's haphazard blasphemy. Hollywood's hatred of God is also apparent in other forms. The elite attack religious people and clergy with a vengeance.

The movie industry would never purposely offend homosexuals, native Americans, environmentalists, animal-rights activists, or women's groups, but they don't think twice about doing something that might offend Christians. In fact, the Hollywood elite seem to get great enjoyment out of trampling our values in the mud. We may never know how many lives have rotted on the trash heap of moral debauchery because of the antimoral anti-Christian perspectives the movie industry calls "art."

Whether or not you attend movies at the theater, you should be concerned about them because sooner or later they will find their way to television and into your living room. What Hollywood sanctions today, the country will probably sanction tomorrow.

Morality in Media reports that the average American household watches seven hours and 41 minutes of television per day. Adults watch an average of four hours and 49 minutes, teens watch an average of three hours and 6 minutes, and children watch an average of three hours and 30 minutes of television per day. In fact, up to 12 percent of television viewers consider themselves addicted to television! This is particularly disturbing in light of the programming currently available.

This is only the tip of the iceberg. You should read our book *A Nation Without a Conscience* to get a more complete picture of how destructive the entertainment and media industries are to the family and our culture. For our purposes here, they are obviously the number-one enemy of the traditional family.

2. *The government—local, state, and national.* One reason we select government as the second most harmful force against the family is a statement Ted Turner made to us in his office many years ago: "Television is more powerful than the government; it elects the government!" We have seen that many times in this country—most recently in 1992, when a man widely known to be a "womanizer" and prevaricator was elected president over a man of character and integrity. Fortunately, the moral devastation brought on by his antimoral policies . . . and those he brought into governmental positions has caused Christians to become so concerned that over 55 percent got involved as responsible citizens in the 1994 elections and voted in a conservative Congress and Senate for the first time in 40 years.

Now the entire nation is waiting to see if these new officeholders, who claim to be deeply committed to traditional values, will live up to their promises and introduce legislation that will have a positive influence on preserving the family. If they do, maybe family-friendly legislation will start coming out of Washington for a change, and the agencies influenced by government will start having a positive influence on individuals, the family, and even our culture.

The story of government's influence on the family is too long to present here (for further discussion, see the author's books *The Battle for the Mind* and *The Battle for the Family*). However, we will highlight three areas that illustrate how government has an incredible influence on the family life of our nation. First is the area of taxes. The main reason 71 percent of American married women work outside the home today is the economic situation created by immoral confiscation of the average worker's income through taxes to finance the destructive liberal socialist policies of the past 40 years. It is well known that the average man has to work until June 10 just to pay his taxes. No wonder mothers have to leave their children with others while they go to work. The harm this does to the family cannot be calculated or justified—particularly when the five trillion dollars wasted on the "Great Society" welfare program has made the problem worse. The problem is compounded annually by the one-third trillion dollars of interest spent on the national debt that has paid for futile programs and a near-equal amount of government waste and "pork" that was never envisioned by the founding fathers.

The second area of government influence on families is the trillions of dollars wasted on the spreading of the religion of secular humanism through our nation's public schools. In addition, they exclude religious history, the Ten Commandments and moral values, and in their place teach such harmful messages as radical and explicit sex education, values clarification, condom usage, and the exaltation of homosexuality.

Third, liberal government leaders have turned the Constitution on its head, reversing the First Amendment, and appointing liberals, atheists, and others who hate Christ, religion, and the church to many of the 748 federal judicial positions, including several on the U.S. Supreme Court. This has made a mockery of our once-great judicial system. Government leaders have failed to regulate the federal airwaves through the Federal Communications Commission, making the government a part of the morally destructive programming of the entertainment industry.

In essence, the government is so busy involving itself in many areas of American life never intended by our Christian founding fathers, that they ignore the areas where they are expected to protect the citizens from the criminal and purulent interests that are destroying us. Pornography is a good case in point. We have gone from a nation with only rare underground access to pornography in 1973, to 1995 where we have become the "pornography capital of the world" as a result of a Supreme Court decision and the failure of Congress to pass corrective legislation. Consequently, this ten-billion-dollar-a-year industry is largely controlled by the Mafia and has produced a drastic increase in forcible rape and an alarming rise in child molestation. Thank you, big government, for helping to destroy the family!

3. *Our governmentally protected, humanistically dominated education system.* When America's educational system was based on the Judeo-Christian values on which it was originally founded, it was the envy of the world and a positive influence on family values. All of that changed as secular humanism (the worship of man through its man-centered philosophy) replaced the Bible with the religion of secularism as the foundation for education.

At one time America boasted the world's greatest system of education, thanks largely to Christians. Harvard, Princeton, and Yale—colleges originally founded to train ministers and missionaries to preach the gospel—were the headwaters of education, providing the nation with qualified educators steeped in biblical concepts for living. About 200 years ago, the Unitarians with their spirit of higher criticism took over Harvard, which eventually became the primary education source for teachers. Toward the end of the nineteenth century, our bright young educators were sent to Europe to get Ph.D. degrees, and they brought back European rationalism, socialism, and existentialism. In the early twenties, John Dewey and his cohorts succeeded in making Columbia University the nation's primary source for educators. As a citadel for atheistic humanism, "anti" everything that is Christian, Columbia gradually took over—ideologically—the nation's school system. Today, the Bible—on which our nation's school system was founded— is the only thing you cannot study in the public school.

Our children are taught everything from evolution to witchcraft at taxpayers' expense, but anything moral, wholesome, or supportive of righteous values is ridiculed. Since many educators believe man is "an animal," they seem obsessed with making him try to live like one. Consequently, free love, drugs on demand, rebellion against society, and anything harmful to the human mind is often advocated or at least presented as acceptable behavior. Currently, the public school system is bankrupt morally, socially, and educationally.

Whenever I review the present status of American education, uninformed parents and naive educators become defensive and take issue with me. But knowledgeable Christians in the secular system verify that I am not exaggerating. In fact, many have said, "You're not telling the half of it." At one time our Christian high school, the largest of its kind in California and perhaps the largest in the nation, took a survey of the professions of the parents who send their children to our school. Would you believe that the number-one answer was "secular education"? In some areas of the country, 30 percent of the public school teachers send their own children to private schools.

Liberal anti-Christian universities produce the journalists, playwrights, communications grads, and so on who work in the media: TV, radio, newspaper, and magazines. Is it any wonder that the media bombards our homes with the same perverted philosophy that subverts our youth in school? A society with a live-like-an-animal mentality will soon destroy itself, and we are rapidly becoming that kind of society. An alarming illustration that the media are more interested in destroying the minds of our people than in making money recently came to light. Last fall, a TV network launched a degenerate program exalting lesbianism, wife-swapping, free love, homosexuality, and every other form of perversion. Ninety percent of the sponsors dropped the show, but rather than admit they had produced a box-office flop, the network castigated the sponsors and went out looking for replacements. Although the top ratings go to clean family shows, network executives seem primarily interested in destroying the last vestige of morality and decency in this nation. People without a strong moral foundation grounded in basic Christian teachings are often deceived by secular entertainment standards, much to their own and the nation's detriment.

We have already seen how harmful media and the entertainment industry have been on our country's moral and family values. Therefore we should ask, "Where did those who control the fare that bombards the minds of our people get their ideas?" The answer is very simple, if you have been trained from kindergarten to Ph.D. degree that "there are no rights and wrongs; everyone has the right to decide for himself what is right for them," you tend to believe it as fact. The public system of education at all levels spews out the culturally destructive message that "there are no moral absolutes." So, as in Old Testament days, "Everyone did what was right in his own eyes" (Judges 21:25). Consequently, we hold secular humanism at fault for the steady decline in the values necessary to maintain good family life and social moral sanity.

The Remedy to Our National Family Breakdown

Those who predict the demise of the family have not reckoned with the power of God. The spiritual renewal going on in the churches of our land is producing a whole new lifestyle, including a wholesome emphasis upon the family. Some of the best family-life instruction that has ever been written is coming from churches and Christian publishers. A recent visit to our local Christian bookstore revealed that books on the family comprise the largest category of new materials and bestsellers. Many concerned individuals outside the church recognize that Christians enjoy the most stable homes in the community and are looking to us for help. The new and growing interest in the family provides today's alert church with the best evangelistic opportunity in decades. The following suggestions provide very practical steps that will go a long way toward stopping the decline of the family.

1. *Win the lost to Christ.* Every evangelistic church can furnish illustrations of an individual who has received Christ and, upon returning to his or her home, watched God gradually transform it. Just last Sunday evening a young father of four shared with our congregation how Christ had changed and revitalized his family since his conversion 18 months ago. Then he proceeded to tell of a business associate he had led to Christ just two days before. Evangelism is the best way I know to refashion the homes of America. Only Jesus Christ can heal the wounds, bind

the hurts, and give the wisdom necessary to raise the kind of children who will produce strong families for the next generation.

2. *Establish a new Christian school system.* The present public school system is so controlled by the federal government and humanistic, even corrupt educators, that there is little hope of salvaging it. In my opinion, the only remedy is for churches and Christians to build a new church-controlled school system in every city in America. I am praying that by the year 2000, at least 51 percent of all educable children in our country will attend a Christian, private, or parochial school that unashamedly teaches biblical principles for living. It will probably take the passage of "school choice"—as advocated by several conservative governors and allowing all parents a voucher of 3000 dollars a year to send their children to the school of their choice—to bring it to pass. However, the conservative landslide victories of 1994 in both houses of Congress may make such a possibility into a national way of life.

3. *The church should register all its members and get them out to vote.* The church needs to do this so that on election day members will vote for those candidates that best support their moral values. The church should encourage Christians to run for public office.

In a free society, voters are responsible for the kind of people who make up their government, from city council to governor to president. Every Christian parent owes it to his children to get out to vote in all elections, so he can give his children the opportunity to grow up in a morally sane society.

The chief reason America has been dominated by humanist or secularist thinkers in government, media, and education during this century is because Christians have been so disinterested in electing the right people to hold office. When I was a boy, the church used to say, "Politics is a dirty business. We Christians should never get involved in politics. We should leave that up to the nice civic-minded people. We should just pray, win souls, and raise our families to love and serve God."

By the fifties it became apparent that those "nice civic-minded people" weren't so nice. Neither were they having a positive effect on our society. The agenda they had, "to make America a secular humanist society," was ruining our culture and even attacking the church. Consequently, some of us began saying that Christians should be more responsible about voting and serving their Lord as government leaders, that evangelicals made up the largest minority in the country and yet were almost totally disorganized. It took a long time, but finally in the eighties Christians began to get the message as our society became more dangerous and immoral. Each election saw more Christians becoming involved.

Finally, in the nineties, particularly 1994, an unprecedented number of Christians ran for public office, many of whom won because for the first time 55 percent of the evangelical Christian population voted. The reason that is important is that 70 to 80 percent of the Christian vote usually goes not to one particular party, but to the candidates who best share biblical moral values. Even secular students of politics who study exit polls acknowledge that the conservative landslide victory of 1994 occurred because of the very high participation of Christians in that election. If that percentage increases as high as 65 percent by the year 2000, we may just enter the twenty-first century with a government that promotes the traditional values this country was founded on, which made her the greatest country in the world.

Since we know personally many of the new leaders in Congress and the Senate, we are convinced we will see a much more family-friendly government in the future. Hopefully, these new leaders will break the stranglehold of liberal humanists who have tirelessly tried to make this a secular instead of a religious-friendly nation, return control of education to local communities, and demand some standard of moral decency for TV and the entertainment industry. It is obvious that the people who have run these industries for years will not clean them up unless forced to do so.

We must make clear here that a conservative government will not usher in the spiritual-moral revival our country needs. That can only be brought about by the prayers and soul-winning efforts of the church. However, a family-friendly government that respects God and religious freedom will create a social climate conducive to the spread of the gospel in this country and through missionary endeavors around the world.

4. *Create a new pro-Christian television and publications network.* Americans need an alternative to the anti-Christian liberalism of the present television networks. Since this is a free country, why shouldn't 50 million born-again Christians and many other millions (possibly another 50 million) have the option of tuning in a channel that will not shatter their moral sensibilities or highlight the bizarre and kinky to the exclusion of the moral and wholesome? Rather than reporting the news, our present networks "manage" it— that is, they present it from their own slanted and often biased perspective. We need an objective network that will give us the true facts about what is going on in our country and world. Our present media system so colors its presentation that Americans have, for most of this century, elected people to office who were far more liberal than themselves.

5. *Pray.* To paraphrase Tennyson, "More things have been accomplished through prayer than this world dreams of." We need millions of people to ask God to forgive our sins and heal our homes. He has saved other civilizations when they turned to Him. Pray for America. There is still

time for God to salvage our nation's moral decline, but it will only come in response to prayer and dedicated work on the part of every believer.

6. *The church should take the lead in family-life training based on biblical principles.* The church is the best-equipped institution of our day to train today's family in the principles that produce a happy and productive home life, for the church bases its teaching on the timeless Word of God, which is the best manual on home behavior ever devised. Consequently, the church should become more aggressive in training its people in Christian family principles and in offering family training to the community. This subject could be effectively used to bring into the church the unsaved in the community who are concerned about family life. There is a new interest in many nonchurched families for some kind of instruction in interpersonal relationships and parenting skills. While we were pastoring in California, we saw many families come to Christ through family-life training.

Chapter 3

The Key to a Happy Marriage

*E*veryone wants to be happy. Perhaps that is why the founders of our country recognized in the Constitution that God has given us the "inalienable right to life, liberty, and the pursuit of happiness." They understand that happiness is worth pursuing—most adults look on marriage as the key to that happiness. That certainly was the case with all the couples who ever came to me as a pastor to get married. Of the 354 couples for whom I have performed wedding ceremonies, not one of them asked to be married because they at last had found the one person who could make them miserable the rest of their lives! Universally, mankind has expected matrimony to usher in that fictitious refrain, "And they lived happily ever after." A quick look at the divorce statistics cited in the last chapter will verify that wedlock is realistically a calculated risk. But we are writing this book to say it *can* be a happily-ever-after experience. With God's power and your cooperation, marriage can become a miniature heaven on earth.

We pause here in our book on the family to focus upon how to have a happy marriage because you can't have one without the other. A couple with unresolved conflicts may beget several children, but they cannot be good parents unless they get along well together. There is no such thing as a happy family without a happy marriage.

While rummaging through over 50 books in preparation for this project, we have noted a variety of keys to a happy marriage as suggested by numerous authors. In my book *How to Be Happy Though Married*, I offer six keys which I have organized into a basic lecture for our seminars. As important as all these keys are, one takes precedence for Christians—the same one that changed our lives and forms the heart of this book. Very simply stated, it is the filling of the Holy Spirit, or the control of the Holy Spirit. They mean the same thing.

In my years of pastoral counseling, I have conferred with over 2500 couples in the throes of marital disharmony. Not once have I had to administer such counseling to a Spirit-filled or Spirit-controlled couple. On several occasions I have pointed out this deficiency in their marriage only to be told, "We used to live like that," and then hear one partner admit, "And we didn't have these problems in those days, either." Very frankly, in our church counseling program we spend little time on symptoms and problems; instead, we concentrate on the Spirit-controlled life. For we have found that if a couple walks in the Spirit, both people can live with or resolve their problems. If they refuse to walk in the Spirit, all the counseling on problem areas and symptoms can be likened to a doctor putting a Band-Aid on a broken leg.

Four Principles to Success in Marriage

Just saying to someone having marital trouble, "You need to be filled with the Holy Spirit," is too simplistic. In fact, it might so irritate them that it makes matters worse. So at the outset we must establish four basic requirements for finding family happiness through the ministry of the Holy Spirit.

1. *You must be a Christian.* The Bible makes it clear that only those who have invited Christ into their lives personally can be guided by His Holy Spirit (Romans 8:9-16). Consequently, if you have not had that life-changing experience, then I would urge you to bow your head and will to Christ and ask Him into your life to forgive your sin and save your soul. Once you have done that, you have become "a child of God" and can proceed to the next step.

2. *Seek biblical instruction by regular Bible reading and study.* God reveals His will to us today through the Bible. It is very difficult to hear His voice among all the worldly voices in society unless we read His Word.

3. *Be willing to do the will of God no matter what it is.* Jesus said, "Blessed are those who hear the word of God and *keep* it!" (Luke 11:28). Just knowing the principles of God is no guarantee of happiness. That blessing is reserved for those who both know His will and obey Him. One of the biggest misconceptions about the Christian life today is that it automatically guarantees success and happiness. I have spent half a lifetime counseling very miserable people, most of them Christians. In almost all cases, they had earned the right to be miserable by disobeying the principles of God that they already knew. You cannot disobey God and expect to be happy. A very strong-willed lady attended one of my seminars and spoke with me afterward to express her displeasure with my formula for happiness. Simply stated, it is: Obeying God's Principles = Happiness.

Evidently, she was disobeying some principle of God (which she would not admit) and refused to give it up even though she and her husband were experiencing a lot of pain in their relationship. Knowing her temperament and her husband's and the way she set her jaw as we talked, I have a hunch she had problems with God's command of submission for the Christian wife (a subject we shall address in a future chapter). Several years later, I heard from her pastor that she was going through a most unhappy divorce. Somehow, I was not surprised.

4. *You must be filled with the Holy Spirit* (Ephesians 5:18). Years ago Frank Sinatra popularized the song "My Way," but that is not the way of happiness for the Christian, which only comes in living life *God's* way. This is what the remainder of this chapter is all about. Many Christians think of the filling of the Spirit as automatic and that all Christians are Spirit-filled. Others think it is optional, and that they can seek the filling of the Spirit if all else fails. Nothing could be further from the truth! Many Christians know almost nothing about the Spirit-filled life and the immeasurable blessings it can provide for them, their family, and their interpersonal relationships.

Bev and I would like to help you in the next few chapters by acquainting you with the biblical instruction that has transformed our lives and marriage. The Holy Spirit is more than willing to empower and beautify your life if, by faith, you are willing to do His will.

The Filling of the Holy Spirit

It is an unfortunate fact that most Christians are confused about the ministry of the Holy Spirit once He comes to live in their lives. Instead of looking into the Word of God to see what He really does in believers, they often look at other people and experiences, which historically have led to confusion. I have met gracious people who had been delivered by the Holy Spirit from some compulsive form of behavior after their conversion but, because of the testimony of other people who had some "experience" they did not have, they assumed "there must be something more" from the Holy Spirit. Other Christians, from a more rigid background, seemed to actually be afraid of the Holy Spirit.

That is why we must briefly study our Lord's teaching about the Holy Spirit to His disciples in John 16. There He makes it clear that it is essential for Him to return to heaven and be with the Father so the Holy Spirit could come and become their helper, comfort, peace, and wisdom. The Lord Jesus came into this world to die for us so that He could "save" us. The heavenly Father planned that entire act—referred to as "the grace of God" or "the mercy of God." Christ is now in heaven interceding with the Father for us. The Holy Spirit is the only member of the Godhead who is constantly with us, for He dwells within us. Success in the Christian life is completely impossible without the ministry of the Holy Spirit.

He is the one who leads us to Christ, convicts us (and the world) of "sin . . . righteousness . . . judgment." He is our source of truth and assurance of salvation, and He leads us to glorify our Lord Jesus Christ in all that we do (John 16:7-15). We are so dependent on the Holy Spirit that we can't even pray properly without Him. For that reason, I hope you see how important it is for you to be acquainted with the Holy Spirit in your life, and with what He will do for you and your family. By this time in your Christian life, I hope you are familiar with the concept that "every good gift and every perfect gift is from above" (James 1:17). The person of the Godhead that provides that "complete" gift (which is what the word *perfect* means) is the Holy Spirit. You and I are not "complete" in the plan of God for our lives until we are "filled with the Holy Spirit." Interestingly enough, as we have seen, that is not optional for the Christian but is the command of God (Ephesians 5:18; Galatians 5:16). No Christian can be controlled by his or her self life and the Holy Spirit at the same time. One will predominate. Either he acts according to his old selfish nature, or he will do deeds that are dictated by the Spirit. And it is easy to tell the difference. If it is self that is in control, the person will be filled with selfishness, anger, fear, or the other "works of the flesh." If the Holy Spirit controls him or her, this person will display the nine fruit of the Spirit.

The Fruit of the Spirit

"But the fruit of the Spirit is love, joy, peace, longsuffering, kindness, goodness, faithfulness, gentleness, self-control" (Galatians 5:22,23). It is impossible for a Christian to be filled with the Holy Spirit and not evidence this filling in some manner. In fact, one of our fundamental presuppositions is this: "When a natural human being is filled with the supernatural power of God's Holy Spirit, he will be different!" As we have pointed out in our books on temperament (see the Bibliography), a Spirit-controlled individual's temperament will not change but will be modified or improved, for his weaknesses will be overcome by the Holy Spirit's power. After carefully studying the 40 most common weaknesses of human beings (ten for each temperament), we are thoroughly convinced that the Holy Spirit provides a strength for every human weakness. Examine the above nine "fruit" or strengths of the Spirit, and you will find one sufficient to overcome every single weakness in your life. Nothing is more practical on a day-to-day basis than the control of our lives by God's Holy Spirit.

As a married woman, do you think you could get excited about going to the door at 5:30 P.M. (or whenever your husband arrives home from work) if you knew that when he opened it, you would be confronted with a man who, in spite of the day's pressures and ordeals, is filled with love, joy, peace, longsuffering, kindness, goodness, and so on? What a marital switch that would be from the usual married man of five years or more who is mentally exhausted at the close of the day. Instead of driving home in the control of the Spirit, he is still nursing grudges, fueling a caldron of resentment, or wallowing in the spirit of self-pity—all of which wring out and exhaust him by the time he reaches his front door. One wife who heard me ask that question replied, "Excited? I'd probably run to the door dressed in boots, apron, and Saran Wrap as Marabel Morgan suggests!"

As a husband, do you think you could get excited at 5:30 P.M. as you pulled into the driveway if you knew that no matter how pressured with babies, broken appliances, and telephone interruptions your wife had been all day, when you opened the door you would discover a woman filled with love, joy, peace, longsuffering . . . ?

The Spirit-Filled Life and Family Living

> Therefore do not be unwise, but understand what the will of the Lord is. And do not be drunk with wine, in which is dissipation; but be filled with the Spirit.
>
> —Ephesians 5:17,18

The above verses provide the most specific command in the Bible related to being filled with the Holy Spirit. Just as a drunk is continually governed by alcohol, the wise Christian will be controlled by the Holy Spirit. Of particular interest, Ephesians 5:17–6:4 contains the most extensive instruction on family living to be found in the entire New Testament. That is why we maintain that the Spirit-filled life is geared to family living, not primarily to church activity. For example, note the structure of the passage:

> 5:18—The command to be controlled by the Spirit
>
> 5:19,20—The three results of the Spirit-controlled life
>
> 5:22-24—Wives are commanded to submit to their husbands

5:25-33—Husbands are commanded to love their wives sacrificially

6:1-3—Children are commanded to obey their parents

6:4—Fathers are commanded to nurture their children

When a Christian family is controlled by the Holy Spirit of God, the wife will submit to her husband, he will love her, the children will obey their parents, and the father will take time to nurture his children in the Lord. Can you imagine a family that lives like that being miserable? Impossible! That is why we have never counseled a miserable Spirit-filled couple. Clearly, the Spirit-controlled life is the real key to exciting family living.

We will highlight other aspects of Spirit-controlled living in later chapters, but at this point it is important to see that the true test of our being filled with the Spirit is how we live at home, not what we do away from the home. If we can live the Spirit-controlled life at home, we can live it anywhere. The pressures that mount in family living certainly surpass any we encounter elsewhere.

One lady misunderstood this fact and inadvertently admitted it when she enthusiastically exclaimed, "I just love coming to this church! I can really feel the warmth of the Spirit of God here. Unfortunately, I don't get that feeling at home. My husband and I are having such conflict that it's impossible for me to be filled with the Spirit there!" Very gently, I acquainted that dear sister with the truth that she was deceiving herself. If she were submitting to her husband, she could easily walk in the Spirit at home, whether or not he was obedient and showed love for her. She could enjoy church because she was free from the home's pressure-cooker atmosphere, where her rebellion against God and her husband continually confronted her. In her case, she was obedient to God in most things outside the home, so she could walk in the Spirit there; but at home she was in defiance of God and her husband. Consequently, mastery by the Spirit was impossible. When she faced her lack of submission as the hindrance to being controlled by the Spirit so she could manifest love, joy, peace, and so on, she quit thinking about the sins of her husband, began to face her own sin of rebellion, and went home controlled by the Spirit. Her husband couldn't believe the change in his wife, and in a few weeks he, too, experienced the filling of the Spirit. As you can imagine, it has transformed their home.

How to Be Controlled by the Spirit

Today there is a good deal of unnecessary confusion about how to be filled with or controlled by the Holy Spirit. Some theologically oriented ministers have made it so mysterious and complex that the average person can neither understand nor enjoy the experience. Other experience-oriented people tell their story with such animation and excitement that the rest of us feel rather inadequate because ours wasn't nearly that thrilling. Besides, they are relating a personal reaction which reflects the temperament and expectations of an individual. For that reason, it is more profitable to look into the Word of God and seek the Bible's teachings, shunning both preconceived ideas and the personal experiences of others.

Surprisingly enough, it is really not difficult to be filled with the Spirit if you are a Christian. (It is impossible, of course, if you're not.) God does not make His commands arduous, nor do we have to beg Him to permit us to do something He has already ordered us to do. We do have to meet His conditions, however, and the major condition to being filled with or controlled by the Spirit is complete surrender to His will. In its simplest form, being filled with the Spirit is a matter of obedience to every decree of God. That is why Spirit-controlled Christians can always be expected to obey the Bible. It is the clearest revelation of God's will. No one can establish a set pattern for implementing the Spirit-controlled life. However, we have shared the following three simple steps with many people who claim He has changed their lives. Hopefully, these steps will prove helpful to you as well.

1. *Examine your life for sin and confess it (1 John 1:9).* The psalmist teaches us that if we harbor sin in our heart, the Lord will not hear our prayer (Psalm 66:18). The first characteristic of the Holy Spirit is holiness. God is holy and cannot tolerate sin. Simply stated, that means we cannot be filled with the Holy Spirit and have sinful practices in our lives at the same time. Several times in our lives we need "sin checks." If you recall attending a communion service you may remember that the Word of God challenges a person to "examine himself, and so let him eat of that bread and drink of that cup" (1 Corinthians 11:28). In other words, we do not rush up to the communion table and partake of the elements, but we first examine our hearts to see if there is sin in our minds or hearts. If we take time to examine our hearts, the Holy Spirit will "convict us" and we will know of that which we should repent. So it is when we prepare to be filled with the Spirit. We must first examine ourselves for all known sin and then confess it.

If you find sin in your life, don't be surprised if that sin fits a habitual pattern of being "the sin that so easily besets" you. All of us, because of our temperaments, backgrounds, and habits, have a tendency to fall into a sin habit or sins to which we are vulnerable. The good news is they can be forgiven and, through the Holy Spirit's power, be overcome. Please keep in mind that your past sins since salvation can be forgiven if you are willing to confess them in the name of Jesus (1 John 1:9). That makes it possible for anyone to be filled with the Spirit who really wants to be and shows that willingness by true confession. Thus, it is important to begin with the confession of all known sin. No one can be filled with the Spirit if he tenaciously clings to a sin habit he is unwilling to forsake.

2. *Surrender your will completely to God (Romans 6:11).* Once cleansed of all known sin, you should tell God formally that you are 100 percent His—that is, you are willing to do anything He instructs you to do. A procedure we have found helpful in this regard is for a person prayerfully to visualize himself lying on an Old Testament sacrificial altar. In your mind's eye picture yourself as a voluntary sacrifice. In this formal dedication you are affirming, "Oh, Lord, I am fully yielded to Your control. I relinquish my mind, talents, family, vocation, money, and future. Please use me to Your glory." It is a very simple procedure, but extremely effective. Be sure to include in particular whatever the Lord has been speaking to you regarding your temper, fears, thought life, ambitions, etc.

3. *Ask to be controlled by the Holy Spirit.* Now that you have met the conditions for being filled with the Holy Spirit, simply ask Him to fill you. Our Lord Jesus admonished us, "If you then, being evil, know how to give good gifts to your children, how much more will your heavenly Father give the Holy Spirit to those who ask Him!" (Luke 11:13).

Many folks have written through the years to tell me how helpful these suggestions are for being filled with God's Spirit. But occasionally, theologians will try to convince me that Christ's promise was given in a different dispensation and is therefore not relevant today. In so doing, they reveal that they have missed the point of our Lord's observation that God is more anxious to impart His Holy Spirit to His children than we parents are to give good gifts to ours. I realize that the promise was given prior to our Lord's experience upon the cross and before the Holy Spirit descended at Pentecost and filled the disciples. The point, however, is that what the disciples needed was the Holy Spirit, and they were taught to ask for Him. The Holy Spirit already indwells us, for we were baptized into Jesus Christ at conversion (1 Corinthians 12:13). But when we are not *filled* with the Holy Spirit, we can be filled in the same way the disciples received Him: by asking.

Frequently, someone inquires at the close of a seminar, "How often should I ask to be filled with the Spirit?" We always reply, "Whenever you think you're not!" If you think you may have grieved Him, ask for the filling of the Spirit the first thing in the morning, several times during the day, and then at night as you drift off to sleep. After a while, it gets to be a part of your life—just like breathing.

What to Expect When Filled with the Spirit

Most of the misunderstanding about the Holy Spirit's work in the life of the believer falls into the category of what to expect. Instead of mentioning the faulty expectations many people have, let us look at the Scriptures. Galatians 5:22,23 lists the nine fruit of the Spirit, or we could call them "results" of the Spirit. In counseling situations I like to call them "strengths," for they provide us the strength to overcome our natural weaknesses. In that vein, look at the first three fruit of the Spirit. They are emotions: love, joy, and peace.

When a person is filled with the Spirit, he will have emotional control. All of us, according to our temperament, background, and life experiences are out of control as far as God's standards are concerned. That is why we sin. But when we are filled with or controlled by the Spirit (which is what "filled" really means), we will have emotional control. And that is what is significant about the control of the Holy Spirit—we are in emotional control. As Paul said in Ephesians 5:18, we are not to be controlled by wine, which makes people lose emotional control. Instead, we are to be controlled by the Holy Spirit, which produces emotional control. As we shall see later in this book, anger—the number-one destroyer of marriage and family life—is an emotion that is brought under control by "love, joy, peace, patience, longsuffering," etc. The same is true for many of the other emotions that easily get out of control due to our natures. These emotions are brought into control when we are filled with the Spirit.

When a natural human being is indwelt by a supernatural power like the Holy Spirit, everyone expects that person to be different. What will be different? He or she doesn't get better-looking or smarter or suddenly acquire a new skill such as playing the piano or painting. The difference is in the person's emotions. The Holy Spirit provides us with emotional control, and that assures us of having control over our out-of-control tendencies. The change in the life of believers that new Christians often talk about is the work of the Holy Spirit on their emotions.

By contrast, when you see a Christian out of emotional control, you know that person is not walking in the Spirit as the Bible commands us. Just as I wrote those lines, Bev hung up the phone to tell me a mutual friend's daughter is being divorced by her husband—"for another woman." Obviously, that couple is not walking in the Spirit, and hasn't been for some time. I remember them when they were "Spirit-filled Christians" (and much happier people, I might add). For some time they have gone their own selfish ways and concluded they no longer loved each other. Yet the first fruit of the Spirit is love. Had they walked in the Spirit as the Bible commands us, they would not be going through a heart-wrenching divorce that also involves two children. Disobeying the Spirit always carries a consequence. In most cases, it is unnecessary unhappiness.

As we shall see in another chapter, we all have different temperaments that make us vulnerable to certain temp-tations and sins, all of which can be overcome by the strength of the fruit of the Spirit, producing both a better and happier lifestyle.

How to Walk in the Spirit

Being filled with the Holy Spirit and walking in the Spirit are not the same thing. Both are essential to the Christian life, and both are commanded by Scripture.

"And do not be drunk with wine, in which is dissipation; but be filled with the Spirit" (Ephesians 5:18). "Walk in the Spirit, and you shall not fulfill the lust of the flesh" (Galatians 5:16). You may ask, "What is the difference between 'walking in the Spirit' and 'being filled with the Spirit'?" Actually, one is the outgrowth of the other. You cannot "walk in the Spirit" (live in the control of the Spirit on a daily basis) until you are "filled with the Spirit." That experience is akin to drinking as much water as you can and then walking in the energy of that life-giving water. Eventually, you will need to drink more so your body will have sufficient fluid to walk farther. And so it is with the Spirit. You will need many fillings of the Spirit in order to walk continually in His control. The following three steps for walking in the Spirit are highly practical principles found in Scripture.

1. *Develop a daily practice of reading the Word of God (Psalm 1:1-3).* The Word of God is to a person what gasoline is to a car. Without fuel, even the most expensive machine in the world will not operate. We have two spirits within us—our own natural spirit called "the flesh," and the new nature called "the Spirit." The one we feed the most is the one which will control us. We do not believe it is possible for a Christian to walk in the Spirit unless he develops the habit of regularly reading the Word to nurture his *spiritual* nature. That is where he gains the spiritual strength to *walk* in the Spirit. He also is given insight into the *ways* of God by reading the Word. As

essential as it is to eat regularly to give you the strength to walk physically in this life, so it is essential to feed your mind on the Word of God daily to gain the spiritual strength to walk in the Spirit on a daily basis.

If you have experienced a difficult time being consistent in Bible study, I have a suggestion for you. Forgive the reference to another of my books, but one of them is a very practical tool I wrote for the San Diego Chargers when I taught their weekly Bible class in our home. Several of them had faced the problem of inconsistency in their daily Bible study, so I developed *How to Study the Bible for Yourself*, a practical guide including nine different charts to aid in Bible study. Since then I have used it to disciple hundreds of men, many of whom found it helpful in producing consistency in their daily spiritual walk.

2. *Develop a keen sensitivity to sin (1 Thessalonians 4:3-8).* Sin is extremely subtle and will keep you from walking in the Spirit. Scripture teaches that God has called us to holiness. Since the Holy Spirit will never lead you in the ways of uncleanness, whenever you become aware that you have begun thinking or practicing sin, you can be sure it was your *flesh* nature, not your *Spirit* nature, that led or controlled you. As you walk in the Spirit, you will become increasingly sensitive to sin and will successfully avoid it more and more. If, however, you ignore that sensitivity to sin you will, of course, be walking in the flesh instead of in the Spirit. You should immediately repent, confess, and be restored to walking in the Spirit. If you reject the Spirit's conviction about your sin, you will gradually sear your conscience and become insensitive to sin, making it easier to walk in the control of the flesh instead of walking in the Spirit.

It is not uncommon to hear of a dedicated Christian who commits some sin that renders him useless in the hand of God. The question invariably arises, "How could he do such a thing?" Very simply—by gradually skipping over the reading of the Word, then by permitting sins to creep into his mind (usually lust, greed, selfishness, revenge, or self-pity). He grieves the Spirit, hardens his heart, dulls his conscience, and sets himself up for the big temptation to which he succumbs. Finally, he is discovered and becomes a "vessel of dishonor." This is why we recommend frequent heart checks, quick judgment of our sins, and daily reading of the Word.

3. *Avoid quenching or grieving the Spirit (Ephesians 4:30-32).* Certain sins grieve the Holy Spirit or stifle His filling of our lives; anger and fear in their many forms are the most common. These, along with their remedy, will be dealt with in detail in the next chapter. Here we will merely point out that a Spirit-controlled Christian will learn to so value the love, joy, and peace which the Holy Spirit brings into his life that he will be watchful lest he grieve Him by the common emotion of anger or quench Him by the equally prevalent emotion of fear.

Major Problems in Marriage: Anger and Fear

*T*he Bible teaches that there are no life testings which are not "common to man." Modern psychology and popular conception would have us believe that each of us, like a snowflake, is singular. Accordingly, many people judge their problem of sin to be unique. My counseling experience, however, has substantiated the teaching of Scripture that sin is "common to man" (1 Corinthians 10:13).

We have already seen that Scripture teaches there is a "sin which so easily ensnares us" (Hebrews 12:1). Personally I have found that, depending on temperament, background, and habit patterns, we may have more than one negative tendency that sets us up for defeat and makes us vulnerable to the devil or the flesh and keeps us from walking in the Spirit. That is particularly true of marriage— the one relationship in life that should provide us with the greatest joy and happiness. Instead, for many couples— even Christians—negative tendencies have brought much misery and heartache. The reason is that their weaknesses collide and often intensify.

As a Christian counselor I have found there are six major problem areas that rob more than half of the couples who marry of the joy God intended for them. We will consider these areas in this and the next chapter. Fortunately, most couples are not plagued with all six problem areas, but almost all couples are vulnerable to some of them. I call these the enemies of the home. You can rejoice because the Holy Spirit can cure all of them if you cooperate with Him on a daily basis.

Have you seriously reflected upon our major premise that "when a natural human being is filled with the supernatural Holy Spirit, he will be different"? Where will that difference occur? The Spirit's filling certainly doesn't make us any better-looking, nor does He impart more talents or a greater IQ. He will, however, enable us to use our capabilities to their ultimate potential, so that in some cases it may appear that He has given new talents to an individual. In reality, He has freed a prisoner from something that has inhibited him all his life.

One of our friends never took a piano lesson, yet he plays the organ and piano beautifully. He cannot read a note of music, but if you sing or play a song for him one time, he can reproduce it. He feels that he was given this gift when he was filled with the Holy Spirit. Actually, he was born with the ability to play music "by ear," but because he is a sensitive and somewhat timid person by nature, his early fears had so imprisoned him that he never seriously attempted to play a musical instrument. After being filled with the Holy Spirit, his natural fears were removed and he became the recipient of that "song in his heart," which we described in the last chapter. In a moment of uninhibited joy, he sat at the piano and, to his own amazement, played a little tune. With practice he has refined that skill until he is most enjoyable to listen to. In fact, he has a particular "feel" about his music that many sight readers lack. The healing of his emotions made him a whole person and set his musical ability free.

Essentially, that is what the Holy Spirit does in a practical sense to each of us when we are filled with Him: He heals our emotions. That is far more significant and relevant for everyday living than most folks realize. What we are emotionally is what we are! A man may boast an IQ of 165, but if he loses emotional mastery, he destroys the effectiveness of his potential. It is safe to say that one's capacity to live up to his potential in life is dependent on control of his own emotions. I have found in counseling that many a severely distraught soul was both gifted and brilliant but could not pull his life together because of lack of emotional control.

Examine the 12 results (or fruit) which the Holy Spirit brings into our lives when we are filled with Him. A song in our heart, a thanksgiving spirit, and a submissive attitude (Ephesians 5:18–21) are all emotional responses, as are the other nine fruit: love, joy, peace, etc. (Galatians 5:22). We associate these good feelings with the heart, and rightly so. Scientists refer to the "heart" as the emotional center of man. The diagram on the following page shows how the heart center is neurologically tied in with the vital organs of the body. Prolonged emotional disorders in the emotional center will eventually take a toll on some part of the body— usually the weakest point. That is what we mean by "emotionally induced illness."

S. I. McMillen, M.D., wrote an excellent book, *None of These Diseases,* from which I took this diagram. In it he listed 51 diseases which people can bring upon themselves due to an emotional upset. Every Christian who reads that book will understand what doctors mean when they say that 65 to 80 percent of all illness is emotionally induced. That is, the patient had nothing organically wrong with him, but his emotional disturbance brought on some ailment. Let's face it: The human body can only stand so much stress before it breaks down at its point of least resistance.

You have probably seen a picture or model at a doctor's or chiropractor's office of the human skeletal system that further illustrates the diagram. From the emotional center (which the Bible calls "the heart") there are white wires that

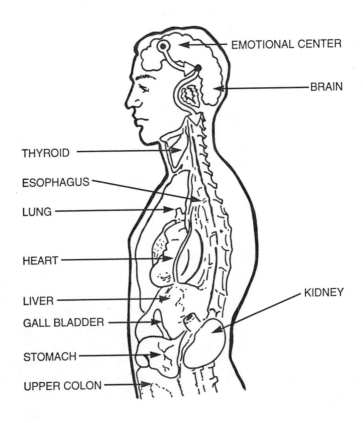

SELF-CENTEREDNESS   ENVY   JEALOUSY   RESENTMENT
HATE   WORRY   OVERSENSITIVITY   GUILT FEELINGS
FEAR   SORROW   DESIRE FOR APPROVAL   FRUSTRATION

EMOTIONAL CENTER

BRAIN

THYROID

ESOPHAGUS

LUNG

HEART

LIVER

KIDNEY

GALL BLADDER

STOMACH

UPPER COLON

Effects of Emotions on Physical Health

ULCERS OF STOMACH AND INTESTINE   COLITIS
HIGH BLOOD PRESSURE   HEART TROUBLE   STROKES
ARTERIOSCLEROSIS   KIDNEY DISEASE   HEADACHES
MENTAL DISTURBANCES   GOITER   DIABETES   ARTHRITIS

represent nerves that run along the spinal column to all the vital organs of the body. If the Holy Spirit controls your "heart" (or emotional center) you are at peace, your whole body is relaxed, and your vital organs function properly. In such a state you will enjoy a long, full life span. However, if you grieve the Spirit by anger or fear or some of the other problems we will discuss that ruin good marriage relations, you cause tension to build up in your heart. This transmits a bad signal through the nerves to the vital organs of your body, causing tension to be transmitted to those organs.

The human body was designed by God as an amazing living mechanism; consequently, it can absorb occasional stress or pressure. But it cannot live with protracted stress. Sooner or later it will break down somewhere, producing some of the 51 diseases Dr. McMillen defined. We have even developed terms that illustrate this process. For example, we have a term "I can't stomach him!" You can't! If you are angry at someone long enough, you can send a bad message along the nerve channel to your stomach and change the chemical balance of your digestive juices so that after they have digested your food they are still powerful enough to attack the lining of your stomach. Doctors call that a perforated ulcer. Another expression we use is "He galls me!" (meaning, "He gets me so upset I send a bad message to my gall bladder and build up stones in that vital organ"). It is incredible how bad emotions over time can ruin good health, from causing high blood pressure, heart attacks, and headaches, to dozens of other physical problems.

In Columbus, Ohio, I spoke on the Holy Spirit's cure for hostility in the home and listed some of the diseases I had seen Christians incur unnecessarily through protracted anger. A young internist came to me registering an interest in what I had taught. He explained that he was an ulcer specialist who received patients only on referrals from other doctors in order to diagnose the cause of their maladies. He said, "As you spoke, I began to think about the five patients

I saw yesterday afternoon. All of them were angry people; in fact, almost all of my patients are angry, hostile people."

Emotions have far more control over our lives than any of us realize, and the Holy Spirit wants to replace our natural weaknesses with His supernatural strengths. You might as well let Him, before these emotions ruin your home life as well as your body—the two most precious assets you own. It is staggering when one tries to imagine how many days a year Christians lie in hospital beds, how many pastoral hours are spent on hospital calls, and how many millions of dollars are wasted by God's people in the "unnecessary illness" category. We could probably build all the new churches and additions to the old ones needed this year with the funds used to pay these medical expenses, if all believers with unnecessary illnesses would be filled with the Holy Spirit and donate their medical savings to the church. But that is nothing in comparison to the happiness it would engender for the homes those Christians represent. Nothing turns young people away from Christ and His church faster than emotionally upset Christian parents. They don't expect Christian parents to be perfect, but they do look for them to be controlled emotionally. That is a reasonable expectation. When parents are filled with the Holy Spirit, they will fulfill that expectation in the home.

Emotional Conflicts: The Cause of Marital Distress

Most couples return from their honeymoon madly in love. They continue that way until they experience their first emotional conflict or clash of wills. We call this "a lovers' quarrel." Usually it isn't fatal, though it leaves a slight scar on their relationship. But making up is such fun! And they hurry down the marital path for another period of time until their next emotional eruption, followed another exciting make-up session. Gradually these conflicts come closer together as the couple's wills and desires clash, and gradually may turn their loving home into a "hell on earth." This may occur before or after the birth of the children, but the situation is rarely improved when the babies arrive. The causes for these nearly inevitable clashes and the role of the Spirit-controlled life in healing them and their causes form the core of this and the next chapter.

No one has to tell a married couple that men and women are different. They are not only built differently, but they also think, feel, and respond differently. Some of that dissimilarity is due to their sexual identity—in spite of what some unisex advocates would have us believe. But much of it due to opposite temperaments.

Why You Act the Way You Do

It is tempting at this point to launch into a presentation of the fascinating subject of the four temperaments, but since we have so thoroughly described them in five of our previous books (see the list on page 232), we shall resist that temptation. It is, however, extremely valuable for the reader to know about human temperament as the best explanation to date of why people act the way they do. Many couples have found it helpful in understanding and accepting their partners, not to mention how it clarifies the reason for their own behavior.

We do not have space in this book to delineate strengths and weaknesses of each of the temperaments. Perhaps you are already familiar with them from our other writings. It is important to point out, however, that our strengths produce our talents and desirable characteristics, whereas our weaknesses provide the inhibiting areas of our lives that often make us undesirable. It is these weaknesses which are overcome by the power of God when we are controlled by His Holy Spirit.

It has been over 25 years since I wrote in *Spirit-Controlled Temperament* that a strength in the Spirit-filled life can be found for every natural weakness. At least 3000 counseling interviews later, I am even more convinced of that fact than I was then.

It has been our observation that opposites attract each other in marriage—not just sexual opposites, but contrasting temperaments. Of the four basic temperaments, it usually happens (though certainly not always) that one of the two extrovert temperaments is attracted to one of the introvert temperaments.

It is important to realize that this rule of thumb is not inviolable. Certainly, in the days when parents selected partners for their children (as they still do in many places of the world), no consideration was given to temperaments. But when individuals make their own selection of a partner, we find that opposites generally attract. The reason is very subtle. We all admire people who are strong in areas in which we ourselves are weak. That admiration, under the right circumstances, often leads to love and the marriage altar. But an unsuspecting newlywed learns soon after the honeymoon that his or her partner isn't perfect after all. And, even worse, he or she is often weak in areas of the other person's strengths. The temptation at that point is to look disdainfully or contemptuously upon a partner's weaknesses or clash with them.

It is imperative that each individual learn to accept his partner's weaknesses along with his strengths and stop aggravating, criticizing, or trying to change him. God alone, with the cooperation of the individual, is able to bring about the desired change. Acceptance of the total person, whether or not you like some of his weaknesses, is essential. Detailed suggestions on how to accept and live with your partner are given in *I Love You, But Why Are We So Different?* For our purposes here, we shall clarify how the six most common emotional problems in marriage often generate conflict, depending on the partners' temperaments. We shall also share a biblical technique for overcoming that weakness which is very practical and has been field-tested in our own lives and in those of hundreds of other couples. The power to overcome these weaknesses, of course, emanates from the Holy Spirit.

The Problem of Anger, Hostility, and Bitterness

Over 80 percent of today's marriages show a predisposition to problems of anger. As one famous marriage counselor told me privately, "Whenever I am at a loss in diagnosing the cause of marital or personal problems, I always look for anger; eighty percent of the time I'm right." We had come to the same conclusion based on our own counseling and because of the fact that three of the temperaments reflect a predisposition to anger. They express it in different forms, but it is anger nonetheless. Sanguines display a quick, hot temper but immediately forget about it after their explosion. Cholerics possess an equally turbulent disposition, but they can carry a grudge indefinitely and burst into flame all over again whenever reminded of what set them off. Melancholies, who are rarely quick-tempered, frequently indulge in revenge. Consequently, they mull things over for a long time, seething inwardly, but may or may not explode. Their pent-up emotions will distinctly inhibit their actual feelings and judgment. Phlegmatics rarely experience anger unless their secondary temperament is sufficiently strong to ignite them. (Most people have two temperaments, a dominant one and a secondary one, and recent temperament tests indicate that some people have three temperaments.) Consequently, some phlegmatics do occasionally experience anger, due to their secondary temperament.

When we speak of anger, we include its various forms of bitterness, revenge, resentment, attack, and perhaps ten other expressions of hostility. In our opinion, nothing is more devastating to a marriage relationship, and no other emotion spoils family living or destroys the psyche of children as does anger. The home was meant to be an emotional haven of peace, love, and joy to which couples and their eventual children could resort, shielded from the hostile, selfish world outside. Unfortunately, many people find more hostility and animosity in their homes than outside them.

Anger is a subtle force which circulates through many people who aren't even aware of its influence. I think of a wife who complained, "I have lost all feeling for my husband." Whenever I hear that lament, I probe for the spouse's trait or habit which upsets her, and it usually does not take long to expose it. In this woman's case, it was his refusal to buy her a $58.95 garbage disposal. When he added insult to injury by saying, "My mother never had a garbage disposal, and I don't see why you need one," she became infuriated. In a matter of weeks her feeling for him had vanished.

This woman was a Sunday school department superintendent and a dedicated Christian wife and mother, but she did not realize that love and hate despise one another's company. Doubtless, this is the reason the Bible so pointedly commands, "Husbands, love your wives and do not be bitter toward them" (Colossians 3:19). In other words, bitterness or love may be expressed, but a relationship cannot admit both simultaneously. This woman confessed her sin of anger, was filled with the Spirit in my office, and went home to love her husband. He could cope with her anger, but all that love finally got to him. One Saturday morning three weeks later he surprised her with a garbage disposal.

One of the most alarming cases of anger I have ever dealt with concerned a young Christian mother who was having flashes of resentment toward her three-week-old baby. She had experienced no such feelings toward her first two little girls, but she tearfully lamented, "I think I am losing my mind and am afraid I might lose control and do something to hurt my son."

It only took a few questions to uncover a bitter, hostile

spirit toward her father, who had been dead for five years. Rather than losing her mind, that woman was letting her pent-up anger construct an emotional current of hatred that was short-circuiting her normal love feelings. All it took to straighten her out was repentance of her sin of anger and the control of her mind by the Holy Spirit so that she no longer dwelt on her father's rejection, abuse, and attempt to molest her. Had she not been able to change her thinking pattern through the Spirit's power, her father would have hounded her from his grave into an emotional breakdown or worse. Such needless tragedies occur every day.

We have dealt repeatedly with people whose inner anger, whether expressed or internalized, has caused such unnecessary tragedies as impotence, frigidity, loss of love, colitis, heart trouble, strokes, emotional breakdowns, and almost every conceivable malady common to man. If you are a regular reader of my books, you probably think I am a bit paranoid about anger because I mention it so frequently, and you may be right. The reason is that I have witnessed countless cases where it single-handedly destroyed health, love, family, children, vocations, and spiritual potential. Very honestly, another reason is that anger came so close to destroying my own family, ministry, and health. Praise God there is a remedy through the Spirit-filled life!

The Cure for Anger

Many people stubbornly maintain that some anger is desirable. Admittedly, Ephesians 4:26,27 allows for righteous indignation, but with three qualifications: 1) do not sin, 2) do not let the sun go down on your wrath, and 3) give no place to the devil. That kind of righteous indignation is impersonal, for it is unselfishly felt on someone else's behalf. The type of anger most people experience, and that which causes the family disharmony we are concerned about, is selfish, pride-filled anger incurred when someone rejects, insults, or injures us.

Currently there is a tendency to offer well-meaning suggestions that we "use our anger," "control it," or "channel it into useful endeavors." As one explosive little lady suggested recently, "Express it!" She mistakenly believes that repressed anger is worse than expressed anger. Actually, expressing anger compounds the problem because it entrenches the habit pattern more deeply into the subconscious mind. Every time we do anything, it becomes easier to repeat the next time as we transform the experience into a habit. That is particularly true of expressing detrimental emotions. Admittedly, repressed hostility can cause bleeding ulcers and the other 50 diseases Dr. McMillen mentions in his book. But there is a better remedy: Cure it! Consider the following steps carefully, for they have been tested and many individuals have verified their effectiveness. You will find these steps to victory over anger similar to those for overcoming the other five emotional problems.

1. *Face anger as a sin (Ephesians 4:30-32).* No sin, habit, or weakness can be overcome unless the individual is willing to face it squarely as wrong. In the case of anger, confronting it as a sin repugnant to God is the first giant step toward cure. If you have any question about anger being wrong, pursue a Bible study on anger. You will find over 25 verses that denounce it, and many illustrations from Cain to Peter that condemn it (none more pathetic than that of Moses). Such a study will help you avoid the natural inclination to justify or excuse your anger. Such action is self-destructive, for it nullifies the possibility of cure. I have never seen a person overcome anger unless he readily admitted it as sin. Uncured anger always limits a person's potential. To fulfill your ultimate destiny and to enjoy marriage and family life to the ultimate, you must gain victory over anger. Anger grieves the Holy Spirit.

2. *Confess your anger as sin (1 John 1:9).* Not only do you need God's forgiveness for your anger every time it occurs,

but you need to verbalize the fact that it is wrong and you wish to be rid of it. God's ear is always attuned to the cry of the sinner, the psalmist tells us, and He is quick to forgive.

3. *Ask God to take away this habit pattern (1 John 5:14,15).* Anger is not merely a sin but a habit. Now that you are a Christian, you are no longer a slave to habit and even have a new power to overcome it. Thus, when anger occurs, acknowledge it as wrong, confess it in the name of Jesus Christ, and enjoy His cleansing. You should also ask for the removal of this habit pattern, knowing that anything you ask within His will He promises to do. Therefore, you can confidently expect this awful habit to *gradually* fade away. Christians may be victims of a habit, but they do not have to be its slave.

4. *Ask for the filling of the Holy Spirit (Luke 11:13).* Every time you sin, it is wise to make this request. Some Bible teachers believe we are automatically refilled with the Spirit the moment we confess our sin, and they may be right. But since I have yet to find a Scripture to prove that, I prefer to ask.

5. *Give thanks for the source of your irritation (1 Thessalonians 5:18).* It is essential that you change your thought patterns about the cause of your anger. That begins by thanking God in and for that circumstance or for that person (Ephesians 5:19,20), realizing that it happened *for* your good (Romans 8:28). It may not have been good in itself, but it happened *for* your good. Be sure you never permit your mind to dwell on that old cause of your anger. If you do, immediately follow this procedure all over again, ending with the giving of thanks.

6. *Repeat this formula every time you get angry.* Habits weren't built in a day, and they won't disappear overnight,

either. But as you use this formula, the incidence of anger will *gradually* melt away. In my own case, I honestly have to admit that once in a while I am still forced to confess a flash of temper, but so less frequently than 30 years ago (about a 300 percent improvement) that it is like being a different person.

A 70-Year-Old Case in Point

Three years after my own filling with the Holy Spirit, I was developing this formula for curing anger and began using it in the counseling room with exciting results. About that time the Lord began giving me invitations to hold meetings in other churches, where I shared these principles (as I do now at seminars) with an overhead projector. One of the first such meetings was held in a little church in Apache Junction, Arizona. At the close of my last message, a rather forlorn-looking man came up and introduced himself as a deacon in the church. "Pastor LaHaye, I wish I had heard this message 40 years ago! I have been an angry person all my life. Is a man 70 years of age too old to try that formula?" To be honest, I didn't really know; I hadn't tried it on a person that age yet. So I prayed quickly for an answer and heard myself reply, "With man this is impossible, but with God *nothing* is impossible to you!" Noticing that he perked up a bit, I added, "The Bible says, 'My God shall supply all your need according to His riches in glory by Christ Jesus.'" Two or three other verses came to mind, and by the end of our discussion he walked away hopefully.

I forgot all about the experience for two years. When I returned to another suburb of Phoenix, I spotted an elderly gentleman and his wife sitting in the evening service and somehow felt that I had met them before. When the service concluded, the man introduced himself as the deacon from Apache Junction. "I just came up to tell you these have been the two best years of my life. I am a different man. If you don't believe it, ask my wife!" I have found that to be the acid test. *What we are at home is what we really are.*

The Problem of Fear, Worry, and Anxiety

Next to anger, the most common emotional problem to strike people, and consequently the family, is fear in its various forms. Fear was the initial negative emotion found in the Bible after Adam and Eve sinned. For the first time man was afraid of the God who loved and made him. Ever since then fear has acted as an emotional destroyer. Dr. McMillen indicates that fear causes the same tensions that are induced by anger; consequently, it is responsible for basically the same 51 physical ailments. The high-pressured pace of the nuclear age in which we live has accelerated the incidence of worry by increasing its causes and lessening many sources of security. The worldwide migration to cities forces man into a competitive environment that is far more conducive to fear than the old rural way of life.

Fear is not usually relegated to a single experience, but becomes a way of life. Fearful people worry about almost anything that is new and different, and some even fuss about things that are familiar. A fearful person will inhibit himself vocationally, socially, educationally, and sexually. In addition, his family and spiritual life will suffer greatly. An associate and I were waiting to be seated at a restaurant for lunch when we noticed a pathetic scene. A dignified phlegmatic man about 50 years old was seated at the counter. When the waitress served his meal and he very softly informed her that it was not what he had ordered, she blew up at him. He was humiliated and offended, but rather than make a scene, he just walked out of the restaurant. My associate turned to me and observed, "That man was my economics professor." In all probability, the good doctor had married a woman who found it equally easy to cow him on every major issue in their marriage.

Everyone experiences fear when confronted by something dangerous or new, but if we let that fear keep us from doing what we should, it is out of hand. Doubtless, you know people who refuse to drive a car but have had ample opportunity to learn. What is the *real* reason they do not learn? Fear. Driving doesn't take special intelligence or mechanical ability as much as it takes enough "nerve" (the term we use to express that which conquers natural fear) to try it. Repetition, however, usually overcomes those fears. Many of our routine activities today caused extraordinary fear the first time we tried them, but our anxiety was kept in check and we proceeded, however uncertainly.

The fear-prone person will not allow himself to do that which arouses fear. We have met several people who were afraid to marry, and others who feared a new job or venture. In the last few years I have taken up skiing, which I thoroughly enjoy. In the process I have confronted a number of folks who are afraid to try skiing, even though the snowy slopes are crawling with four and five-year-olds. Most of those who inhibit themselves by fear develop an ability to think up good excuses why they shouldn't do anything. Every local church recognizes that a large number of its membership have never taught Sunday school or summer Bible school, participated in the visitation program, or involved themselves in any of the many programs. The real culprit (their ingenious excuses notwithstanding) is fear. More Christians fail to take advantage of witnessing opportunities because of fear than due to any other reason. Almost every Christian I have met would love to share his faith and lead others to Christ, but fear may seal his lips.

Fear stifles conversation and communication in the home. It hampers many parents from insisting on standards and guidelines, and it occasions many family squabbles. We have watched sadly through the years as good parents made the fatal mistake of being afraid to discipline their teenage children. In fact, Bev and I have come to the conclusion that the most common mistake Christian parents of teenagers make is letting them pick their own friends. It can be fatal! All the good teaching of their young years goes down the drain when a young person selects carnal or unsaved teens as his dearest friends. Before long the Christian teen looks and acts like the teen from a non-Christian home. The youth at church somehow lose all charm to the now-carnal Christian, even though he grew up with them as his best friends. He is simply no longer on their spiritual wavelength. Tragically, many parents know the biblical principle that "evil company corrupts good habits" (1 Corinthians 15:33), but are afraid to say "No!" "Stop!" or "Quit!" Why? Fear. Fear that their teen won't love them or will leave home. Ironically, they usually lose the very one their fear keeps them from trying to save.

What causes people to be fear-prone? Any explanation logically begins with their basic temperament. Phlegmatics are anxious worriers; melancholies are fearful of criticism, injury, insult, and fear itself. A person who is part melancholy and part phlegmatic will, of course, be both fearful, worrisome, and insecure. Cholerics are rarely fearful unless they possess a high degree of melancholy or phlegmatic as a secondary temperament. In *Understanding the Male Temperament*, where I develop the 12 blends of temperament, I call those people ChlorMels or ChlorSans. The sanguine, like the choleric, isn't usually afraid of anything and may even be a daredevil, but he is insecure and so loves to please other people that he becomes fearful about gaining or maintaining their approval. Fully half of the temperament blends could produce a fear-prone person.

Temperament alone does not fully account for a person's fears, worries, and anxieties. It does, however, provide him with a predisposition toward mental anxiety which can be eased considerably by love, discipline, and security in the home, followed by strong spiritual growth. The same basic temperament subjected in childhood to rejection, lack of discipline, or unreasonable dominance without the aid of spiritual development will produce a fear-ridden adult. Add to this the possibility of traumatic childhood experiences, a negative thinking pattern, and several other fear-producing factors, and you have a real fear case on your hands.

Anger Versus Fear in Marriage

We have already seen that warm, personable sanguines are often drawn in marriage to cool, rigid, perfectionist melancolies. On the other hand, the quick, hot choleric tends to prefer the calm, easygoing, never-get-upset phlegmatic. Those are perfect formulas for collision and catastrophe in marriage because the fear inhibitions of one temperament cause disagreements with the other. The fears of childhood are frequently overcome during the courtship stage through love, libido, and excitement. However, they gradually return after the honeymoon is over and the routine of daily living sets in. Within weeks or months the fears of one spouse collide with the anger of the other. If the partners are not unusually unselfish people, their genuine love will begin to tarnish, and eventually they may deem their "incompatibility" grounds for divorce. But remember that incompatibility is a *result*, usually of fears and anger in collision. In *Understanding the Male Temperament* I discuss at length how a couple can generally adjust to each other's opposite temperaments. Here, however, I would like to show God's cure for the fear problem. For even if a husband or wife learns to adjust to a spouse's anger and fear, that will not solve the fear problem which inhibits the fearful partner in many areas of life.

The Cure for Fear

Don't be disappointed if you find the cure for fear almost identical to the cure for anger. Both are temperament-induced tendencies which, through the circumstances of life, have turned into a deeply entrenched habit pattern. With God's help you will cure the habit of fear, worry, and anxiety the same way you cure any basic habit.

1. Face fear, worry, and anxiety as sin (Romans 14:23).
2. Confess worry, fear, and anxiety as sin (1 John 1:9).
3. Ask God to take this habit pattern away (1 John 5:14,15).
4. Ask for the filling of the Spirit (Luke 11:13).
5. Thank God for who and what He is and what He can supply in your life as you face this problem (1 Thessalonians 5:18).
6. Repeat this formula every time you become fearful.

Bev's Story

Since I have already acknowledged that I was the angry one in our relationship, you might have guessed that Bev inherited a natural fear problem. Unlike many couples, we were filled with the Spirit the same week, so both of us began the process of change at the same time. As my sinful habit of anger was being replaced by the Holy Spirit's love, peace, and self-control, Bev's fears, worries, and insecurities were being modified by faith, peace, love, and self-control. This, of course, did wonders for our marriage. It also transformed Bev's ministry. Previous to being filled with the Holy Spirit, she had limited her ministry to children under the level of the sixth grade. Although she was the best junior-department superintendent I had ever seen, she would never address adults. Gradually, she began accepting speaking opportunities at women's conferences and banquets, and today she ministers dramatically to large women's groups and even mixed audiences in our Family Life Seminars. I have watched a beautiful rosebud, once confined by her own fears and anxieties, blossom out into a full-blown flower of poise, radiance, and Spirit-controlled confidence. But God still wanted to do a special work in her.

The director of a mission board wrote to thank me for writing *Spirit-Controlled Temperament*, which he said was "required reading for all our missionary trainees. There is just one problem with it. You tell how God delivered your wife from her fear of public speaking, but later admit she couldn't join you and the rest of the family in waterskiing because she was afraid of the water. The problem is that our non-swimming missionary candidates readily identify with her and use her as an excuse for not learning to swim, which could prove fatal to some of them." He went on to graciously ask, "Isn't the fear of water just as much a sin as the fear of anything else?"

I thought about that letter for two days and then took it home and asked Bev to "sit down. I have something for you to read." As she began reading, I went into the next room and got her the Kleenex box, which she needed. Several days later I heard her on the phone talking about "swimming lessons." She cleverly lined up a heated swimming pool and a phlegmatic instructor. Dressed in my rubber wet suit (which I wear in the winter for waterskiing—it not only keeps you warm but also makes it impossible to drown), she also strapped on a life belt. Arming herself with her New Testament, she quoted: "I will never leave you or forsake you," and other verses on assurance of God's provision. Eventually, she was able to discard the unnecessary paraphernalia and learned to swim. She will never be a U.S. Olympic candidate, but she conquered her terrible fear of water.

Last summer while the family was enjoying our annual waterskiing trip at Lake Powell, I stood on the back of our rented houseboat and looked down at her swimming in water 175 feet deep and thought, "Who but Jesus Christ by His Holy Spirit could replace obsessive fear with relaxing faith?"

An Overcoming-Fear Update

Since writing the above, I have witnessed further evidence of the Holy Spirit's power to overcome an ingrained fear habit. In 1979 I organized a rally in the Long Beach Auditorium for pastors and concerned Christians in opposition to the liberal humanist trends that were spreading across our state and corrupting our society, schools, and cities. Among the speakers that day I introduced Beverly— the woman who just a few years before had been afraid to give a devotional to eight women in our own church—to a crowd of 7000 men and women. She went on to found Concerned Women for America (CWA), which became the largest pro-family women's organization in the country. Now located in Washington, D.C., CWA has almost 700,000 members. I have seen her, at the request of two U.S. presidents, speak on behalf of conservative Christians in favor of three United States Supreme Court appointments. The first was Judge Antonin Salia, the second involved the controversial and very scary appointment process of Judge Robert Bork, where her testimony was carried on national TV, and later on behalf of Judge Anthony Kennedy. She was even prepared to speak up for conservative judge Clarence Thomas during the national attack of the feminists and Anita Hill on his nomination.

My point is not to exalt Bev; God has done that. She has graciously represented Christian women in the public press and media now for several years. As the nation's most-listened-to daily radio "talk-show" hostess, she had a powerful impact in informing and mobilizing the largest number of Christians in history to get out to vote on election day, November 8, 1994 (which may go down in history as the day conservative citizens broke the 40-year stranglehold liberals had on the American government and people). My real point is, where did the power to overcome her natural fear, worry, insecurity, and lack of self-image come from? Be sure of this: It didn't come from turning over a new leaf or through a resolution! It came from the Holy Spirit who gave her faith for her fears, plus courage and self-control.

A federal judge spoke to me after I addressed a group of men at a Maximum Man conference in Louisville, Kentucky, to say, "Would you give a message to your wife from me?" Then he said, "I saw her testimony on behalf of Judge Bork on CSpan TV—I thought she was superb!" If God's Spirit can make a formerly frightened phlegmatic/sanguine introvert (with a tad of melancholy and a shade of choleric) into a "superb" witness in front of liberal senators Ted Kennedy, Joe Bidden, Howard Metzenbalm, and five other antagonistic liberals, surely He can calm your greatest fears or angers and supply all your needs—just as He promised.

Chapter 5

The Number-One Problem in Marriage

*T*he number-three bomb in the arsenal of marriage problems is basic to all mankind: selfishness. We are all born with it, and to one degree or another it plagues us throughout life. In our opinion, one of the chief responsibilities of parents is to train their children away from selfishness. Every baby comes home from the hospital with the self-centered attitude that he is the only child on earth. Any perceived need for food, sleep, or a diaper change will occasion a howl of protest: "I want attention now!" We accept that as normal because he is immature. But unless trained out of it through years of love and discipline, he will still be immature at 20 years of age and will serve as a bad risk for marriage. A candidate for matrimony should look carefully at the "unselfishness quotient" of the partner-to-be. If he is unselfish, his anger or fears will be kept in better check, and any other undesirable characteristics will be more easily overlooked. The hardest person to love over a period of time is not one who is unattractive or possesses a zero personality, but a partner who is selfish.

An egocentric person thinks of himself first and foremost in everything. Consequently, he finds giving and sharing difficult habits to cultivate. All temperaments have their own tendencies to be selfish, but some are by nature more easily trained out of them. A sanguine is selfish about his person, for his giant ego requires that he remain the center of attention at all times. Cholerics selfishly run roughshod over others or use people for their own purposes, then cast them off when they are through. Melancholies are prone to be self-centered and evaluate everyone from the standpoint of what is good for themselves. Phlegmatics are overprotective of themselves, often afraid they will be hurt or offended, and they are apt to be stingy.

Selfishness Is a Loser

Happiness is dependent on learning to share one's self, time, talents, and possessions with others. Ideally, love overcomes selfishness during the courtship days and often throughout the honeymoon. But gradually a person's basic selfish habits return, and love dies proportionately. For that reason, money problems arise quickly in the marriage—so frequently that many counselors call this the chief difficulty in matrimonial adjustment. Methods of handling money fairly and frugally are important, but improved methods never change a selfish heart; they just make it easier to live with Mr. Selfish.

Money is only one subject which is distorted by selfishness. Others include children, parents, holidays, sports, hobbies, lovemaking, churchgoing, giving, and most other facets of living.

The Bible offers extensive comment on selfishness. Consider the following examples:

> [Jesus' Golden Rule:] Whatever you want men to do to you, do also to them (Matthew 7:12).
> Give, and it will be given to you: good measure, pressed down, shaken together, and

running over will be put into your bosom. For with the same measure that you use, it will be measured back to you (Luke 6:38).

But whoever has this world's goods, and sees his brother in need, and shuts up his heart from him, how does the love of God abide in him? (1 John 3:17).

Let nothing be done through selfish ambition or conceit, but in lowliness of mind let each esteem *others* better than himself. Let each of you look out not only for his own interests, but also for the interests of others (Philippians 2:3,4, emphasis added).

True love and giving all of yourself and your possessions to those you love are inseparable. Love is not static; it is an emotional motivator which causes a person to give. Love may well reside in a selfish person's heart, but it may be blocked by self-love. As we shall see in a later chapter, our love priorities should be: 1) love God supremely, 2) love our partner and family, and 3) love our neighbor as ourself.

The Cure for Selfishness

The same basic cure for anger and fear will work for selfishness, so I will leave it to the reader to enlarge and apply the following abbreviated steps:

1. Face selfishness as sin.
2. Confess it.
3. Ask God to take away this habit.
4. Ask for the filling of the Spirit.
5. Thank God for His love that is flowing through you to make you a more generous person
6. Repeat this formula each time you do, say, or *think* anything that is selfish.

Gradually this habit pattern will begin to fade, and a mature generosity and true love for others will replace it. Your patience toward people will also be extended; you will increasingly enjoy others, and they will begin enjoying you. Philippians 2:3,4, cited above, emphasizes the words *other* and *others*. A mature, unselfish person never lacks for friends, for he is so "others" conscious that they recognize it and feel comfortable in his presence. In the family, such a person is a delight to have around the house. Instead of being interested in his own rights or possessions, he develops "others" awareness.

The key word here, of course, is *gradually*. Don't expect an instant cure for selfishness—or for any sinful habit or tendency. Habit is a cruel taskmaster, and although we Christians are not "slaves to habit" as are non-Christians who do not have the indwelling power of the Holy Spirit, we are, nevertheless, often victims of habit. It is unrealistic for a selfish person or for the spouse of a selfish person to think that one experience of being filled with the Spirit and following the above formula will cure them of selfishness (or anger, fear, or any other sinful practice). That will only come as they gradually (and persistently) face every selfish action as sin, and follow with confession and the rest of the steps in the above formula every time the sinful habit occurs. I should know. My pet sin, as I have said, was anger, which is a form of selfishness. I had to use that formula at least 95 times the first day. Things were much better the second day (I only had to use the formula 91 times). I can't say I never get angry today, but anyone who knew me back in my angry days will tell you I am a different man. If you don't believe it, ask my wife!

Most Christians who fail to gain victory over selfishness or other sins do not fail for lack of sincerity but for lack of persistence. They give up at the first signs of failure. Stirring up feelings of failure is a tactic of the devil. He doesn't want Christians to have lasting victory over sin;

consequently, he inspires feelings of defeat when habit rears its ugly head, and you revert to selfish behavior. The only way to lick him at his game is to immediately repeat the above formula every time you need it.

How to Live with a Selfish Mate

Selfishness is indeed the chief cause of marital disharmony, and all too often ends in divorce. However, I do not find that the Bible condones divorce in response to selfishness. Adultery, yes. Selfishness, no. So what is a Christian mate to do if a selfish partner is unwilling to face his or her sin and seek God's help in overcoming it? The answer is not to go see your lawyer; it is to ask the Holy Spirit to flood you with His love, joy, peace, etc. You will find that He will give you sufficient grace to live with your selfish companion. Since He promised to supply all your needs, you can depend on Him to supply grace to love, honor, and cherish that person—just as you promised to do at your wedding altar.

In the counseling room I have had people say, "But you don't know how selfish my partner is!" That may be true, but I do know the grace of God. The Bible guarantees it will be sufficient, that God will provide all you need. Trust Him! Walk in the Spirit and let God take care of your partner. You can only make decisions like that for yourself. And whether your partner decides to stay with you in a selfish mode is his or her decision. Your decision should be to trust God, take Him at His Word, and walk in the Spirit. Each time you get angry at your spouse's selfishness, confess your anger and commit him or her to God. Then watch what God will do. He is a master at transforming lives. If, however, their selfishness leads to adultery or abuse, that injects other biblical principles that must be considered. Counseling by your pastor in such cases is definitely advised.

One thing the spouse of a selfish mate should do is seek a good time to have a loving confrontation for, as the

Scripture says in Ephesians 4:15, "speaking the truth in love." You can walk in the Spirit and graciously confront another person's sin. Actually, Scripture admonishes us to do so. There are several reasons for doing so, one of which is so the person will know you do not approve of the behavior. There are a surprising number of partners who never confront their mates, assuming, as several have confided, "I just think he should know he is offending me." Selfish people are usually quite insensitive. Make sure you tell them—"in love." Another reason you should confront a selfish mate is because if you don't, the pressure will build up in you until you explode in anger. Then you will not only "grieve the Spirit," but you will also say too much too harshly and end up doing more damage than good.

Once having confronted the person "in love," you then can commit the partner to God and expect Him to work on your spouse. Trust me. Better yet, trust the Word of God. He will!

The Problem of Infidelity

Since earliest times, the misuse of man's God-given sex drive has proved to be a major human problem. The Holy Spirit was obviously aware of that fact, for in His list of 17 common "works of the flesh" (Galatians 5:19-21) the first four are sexual sins: adultery, fornication, uncleanness, and licentiousness. They were problems in Israel, the Corinthian church was plagued with them, and rampant sexual vice is predicted for the last days. If we are indeed in the last days, we can expect the appetite for immorality to increase.

In the early days of our ministry, we were occasionally confronted by various kinds of unfaithfulness among couples, from incest to homosexuality and back through all conceivable forms of fornication, even among church families. For reasons already given, the forms of temptation have increased, and the number of Christians falling into these sins has risen alarmingly. On many occasions we have been brought in to help pick up the pieces of people's lives destroyed by such infidelity. God's grace is sufficient to put things back together, but immorality usually leaves scars that only years of faithfulness can erase.

God's plan for marriage has always been one man for one woman, as long as they both live. Anything short of that is a sin against God and a betrayal of the trust of your dearest friend. Faithful partners, we may add, are not untempted partners. The decline in moral values, from actors on TV to government leaders, during the last 20 years has made matters worse. Marital temptation has increased in direct proportion to women entering the work-place. In addition, aggressive sexual behavior, due largely to the emphasis in TV programming, has graphically increased the problem. Almost every red-blooded person has had opportunity to cheat on a mate, but most reject such temptation through love, honor, and commitment. Giving in to such temptation usually creates more problems than the tempted person ever imagined. The resultant load of guilt and shame is often overpowering. We have counseled many couples six months or a year after their sin and found that it still occasioned sexual maladjustment problems not experienced previously. The wages of all sin are much too high, and that is particularly true of sexual sins.

The Cure for Infidelity

The practice of immorality, interestingly enough, is easier to break than the emotional sins cited earlier, for two reasons. First, it is so blatantly sinful that only an extremely strong-willed, carnal Christian denies it is sin (after he gets caught). In the last few years, however, some Christians have actually tried to tell me they were Spirit-filled while living away from their wife and with another woman. Most Christians, however, recognize such activity as sin. Self-deception is simply the result of a long-standing sin pattern. Second, it is easier to gain victory over sexual than emotional sins because no habit pattern is involved. Sexuality is a physical function that takes two people. But the habit of mental-attitude lust must be cured before lasting victory can be obtained.

Our Lord demonstrated His understanding of human nature when He spoke ("For He knew what was in man"—John 2:25), but never more so than when He said, "Whoever looks at a woman to lust for her has already committed adultery with her in his heart" (Matthew 5:28). The Christian who never commits mental-attitude lust will never commit adultery. Even though the secular world of psychology commonly suggests that sexual fantasies are normal (the everyone's-doing-it routine), they are wrong. This premise lies in direct conflict with the teaching of Jesus Christ. As one of the Scriptures already quoted about the Holy Spirit teaches, "For God did not call us to uncleanness, but in holiness" (1 Thessalonians 4:7), and this begins in the mind.

The people of Noah's day were sexual degenerates whom God destroyed because "every intent of the thoughts of his heart was only evil continually" (Genesis 6:5). Such thought patterns are easily ignited today by the increase of pornography, X-rated movies, and so on, but no Christian man or woman has to be in bondage to such sin. He that is in us is greater than he that is in the world (1 John 4:4). Therefore, we need not become slaves to sin. In addition, it is almost unnecessary to add that no one whose mind is filled with lustful thoughts can be filled with the Holy Spirit. The following six steps to overcoming infidelity, or the adulterous lust thoughts that produce it, will provide a cure *before* those thoughts inspire the intense feelings that lead to marriage-jolting sin:

1. Admit that all lust thoughts and adultery are sin (Matthew 5:28).

2. Confess them each time they occur (1 John 1:9).

3. Ask God to take away the pattern and cleanse your mind (1 John 5:14,15).

4. Ask for the filling of the Spirit (Luke 11:13).

5. Thank God for His victory and concentrate on pure thoughts (Philippians 4:8).

6. Repeat this formula each time you indulge lustful thoughts.

Doctors of the mind and students of human nature tell us that 21 days of abstinence will break a habit. I tried it on coffee one time, assuming they were right (to prove to myself I could break the habit), then returned to it on the twenty-second day because I enjoy the taste. Their prescription may work for habits, but personally I think it takes longer than that when we attempt to train the mind or control our thoughts. It is verified in 2 Corinthians 10:5 that we *can* bring our thoughts into obedience to Christ. In the case of someone who has been practicing the habit of mental-fantasy lust for a long time, the frontal lobe of his brain (the thinking, reasoning, and remembering bank) is saturated with lustful thoughts in living color. It will take at least three to four months of pure-thinking days to force those memories (even if only fantasies) to recede to a less influential part of the mind.

One man I worked with for over a year fought an intense battle with lust. He finally cured his problem by fining himself each time he regressed. His self-chosen fine was to memorize a verse of Scripture. The last time I talked to him, he was reviewing a packet of 129 Scripture cards. Why was he victorious? Because he meant business.

Married Lovemaking

The Bible teaches that one of the major purposes for the act of marriage is for mutual pleasure and the lessening of sexual temptation. Marital lovers enjoy the intimacy, warmth, and fulfillment of sexual ecstasy, followed by the afterglow of fulfillment and rightness, because it is approved by God. No clandestine affair can ever equal such a sexual experience because an affair is followed by guilt. If you have difficulties in your marital love life, we recommend our book *The Act of Marriage.* It was designed to help all Christians learn the art of mutual sexual satisfaction that 85 percent of the Spirit-controlled couples we polled enjoy. This not only enriches their relationship to each other, but also serves as a safeguard against moral infidelity.

The Problem of Self-Rejection

In recent years we have been alerted to the universal problem of self-rejection. Unlike the problems we have already discussed, this emotion is not always readily apparent. Instead, it may be so deeply internalized that it goes unrecognized because it adopts so many faces, which vary with the individual and the occasion. Self-rejection can cause a person to retreat socially and vocationally, check the expression of his personality, indulge in self-deprecation, concede inferiority, fall into depression, or succumb to a host of other misconceptions—some quite bizarre. At best, self-rejection incites capable people to sell themselves short in life.

There are many causes for self-rejection, including temperament, but the most important involve parental disapproval, criticism, and rejection. Usually the child who is given love and warmth in the home, particularly during the early stages of life, does not have a problem with self-rejection unless he has a strong melancholy temperament. One of the weaknesses of the melancholy is his spirit of criticism, which he often uses on himself. The Spirit-filled life is the only remedy for this.

In *How to Win Over Depression,* I go into detail on this subject, so I will not belabor the point here, except to list the general causes and cure. Most people reject their appearance, talents, environment, parents, or future. Few people reject all five. If they do, of course, they are in serious trouble. Those individuals who have read our books may add one more area of rejection: their temperament. Regardless of the temperament combination they possess, they are certain that they would be happy had they been something else. Actually, as I have noted on several occasions in print or in public, no one temperament or combination of temperaments is better than another, though some are better than others for *certain things*. For example, I don't think I would go to Dr. Sanguine if I thought I had something seriously wrong with me. As a pilot I might see him for a quick medical exam to satisfy the Federal Aviation Administration, but if I were suspicious that I had a serious ailment, I would see Dr. Melancholy or Dr. Phlegmatic. (Dr. Choleric is usually too rough. By the time he gets through probing or jabbing the tender area, the problem has gotten worse. He is excellent, however, during war-time as a battlefield doctor, or as supervisor of the emergency ward in some big hospital, where the situation often calls for snap decisions.)

The Cure for Self-Rejection

The self-rejecting individual must first come to realize that he is in defiance of God. When we dislike our looks, body size, temperament, or talent, whom do we blame? God, of course. He is the One who arranged at conception the genes that produced us. Many people have said or implied, "I don't care what you say; if God loved me, He would not have made me this way." Such thinking is not only sinful but will also lead to sickness, thus compounding the problem. Only by facing their ingratitude, unbelief, and rebellion against God will such individuals learn to accept themselves. The following steps apply our method of cure to self-rejection:

1. Face and confess self-rejection as sin.
2. Ask God to take away the habit of self-rejection.

3. Ask Him for the filling of the Spirit (Luke 11:13).

4. Thank Him for who and what you are (1 Thessalonians 5:18).

5. Repeat this formula each time self-rejection occurs.

6. Look for an area to serve God and others (Romans 12:1,2).

It is particularly important that Christian self-rejecters thank God *formally* at least one time for who and what they are. If appearance is your subject of rejection, then look at your reflection in the mirror and thank God for how you look, particularly those areas you have been rejecting. Remember, if God had wanted you to look otherwise, you would. Then thank Him for your talents and offer them to Him. Even if you consider your gifts as only minimal, He is a master at taking ordinary people and doing superordinary things with them. I can certainly vouch for that. If I told you my high school and college English grades, you would probably stop reading this book immediately. If you saw my penmanship, you probably couldn't make out half the words. Our God has never been limited to using only talented individuals, and since He is the Source of all power, let Him flow through you. Everyone will be amazed at the result.

You might wonder why I include self-rejection in this list of family enemies. I agree with Bill Gothard, who said, "A person's attitude toward himself will influence his attitude toward God, others, and everything he does." To function at your maximum efficiency, you must realize that you are important enough for God to let His Son die for you, and that God wants to use your life, beginning in your own home.

Many well-meaning Christians cling to the mistaken notion that self-acceptance or love for self is unspiritual. Admittedly, one fruit of the Spirit is "meekness," but our

Lord assumed self-acceptance when He said, "Love your neighbor as yourself." God's divine order is clear: Love Him supremely, then your partner and children, and finally your neighbor and yourself equally. If you depreciate yourself, it will keep you from loving your family as you should. An excellent book on this subject is James Dobson's *Hide or Seek*.

The Problem of Depression

Fifty thousand to 70,000 annual suicides due to depression verify the seriousness of this problem in our culture. Any Christian counselor will testify that it is one of the most common disabilities he confronts. Because many Christians refuse to seek the aid of counselors, they try to live with the pain (like they would with a low-grade infection in the body), as if it were a necessary part of life.

Depression was saved for last not because it is the least important problem, but because it is a result of anger, fear, and self-rejection. The many symptoms and causes are detailed in *How to Win Over Depression*, which should be helpful to those who are plagued by this enemy to happy family living. I wish to point out that a cure *does* exist. I am convinced that Spirit-filled Christians (except for those very rare few who develop a biological cause, or are genetically predisposed to depression that only medication can cure) will not be depressed. In fact, depression should serve as a warning that a person needs to see a doctor or that he or she is not filled with God's Spirit but permeated with self.

The problem of depression can be cured quite readily if the person is willing to face what causes it. But many strike out right there. The real problem for the 98+ percent who do not have a biological cause for depression is *self-pity*. Every time a person uses any of the common reasons for indulging in self-pity, he begins to get depressed. You can actually chart your own depression, for its intensity will vary with the degree of self-pity. The time sequence is also important.

Usually within 1 to 24 hours after someone inaugurates the process of self-pity, he becomes aware of the depression. Those who have nurtured self-pity for years (until they are quite skilled at it) may be able to feel its effects in a matter of minutes.

Depression never starts without provocation. A happy, well-adjusted person will not suddenly become depressed, as if he were hit by a viral infection. Usually he will find that something specific happened or will remember a previous unfortunate event—perhaps rejection by someone he loves, an insult, or an injury. The following depression-producing formula should be cemented in your mind. Any time you find yourself drifting into depression, think of this formula and then follow the steps for a cure.

$$\left.\begin{array}{l} \text{Rejection} \\ \text{Insult} \\ \text{Injury} \end{array}\right\} \text{SELF-PITY = DEPRESSION}$$

The Cure for Depression

1. Face self-pity as a mental sin pattern.
2. Confess this sin of the mind.
3. Ask God to take away this thought pattern.
4. Ask for the filling of the Holy Spirit.
5. Thank God in the midst of the rejection, insult, or injury that He is with you, supplying all your needs.

$$\left.\begin{array}{l} \text{Rejection} \\ \text{Insult} \\ \text{Injury} \end{array}\right\} \text{Thanksgiving by Faith = JOY}$$

6. Repeat this formula each time you find yourself depressed.

The Key to Depression-Free Living

The formula for depression-free living shown above reveals that the harmful emotion of depression, that has literally broken the health of many people, is the result of a bad mental attitude. We have a common expression today that describes many people who exhibit abnormal behavior. We say, "They have an attitude problem." This mental-attitude problem not only prompts some people to drive recklessly, endangering others' lives, but it can also lead to outright violence and even murder. If we can change the attitude, we can change the be-havior. That principle also applies to depression. If with God's help we are able to get a depressed person to change his mental attitude, he will experience the lifting of the depression.

That is why I stress in point 5 above the giving of thanks, which I believe is the key to lasting victory in this arena. We *can* control our thoughts. In fact, the Bible commands us to in 2 Corinthians 10:5. The problem is, the mind can't stop thinking (or we're dead). For practical purposes, we just can't start thinking self-pitying thoughts or we will again take up that harmful, self-centered lament. Instead, we must fill our minds with something positive. And that is where thanksgiving becomes so helpful. By casting down self-pity and replacing these harmful thoughts with thanksgiving, as the Bible commands us, we gradually heal our depressed feelings. The key to depression-free living is, *"In everything give thanks; for this is the will of God in Christ Jesus for you"* (1 Thessalonions 5:18).

The Spirit-Filled, Happy Home

At great length we have dealt in the past two chapters with what we consider the six most prolific problem areas facing Christian families today. All of these problems grieve or quench the Holy Spirit and limit His use of our lives. If you find one or more of these problems cropping up in your life or family, discuss it with your partner and follow the recommended procedure for cure. Any home so filled with the Spirit that the members almost never see one of these enemies attack will enjoy a song in the heart, a thanksgiving attitude, a submissive spirit, love, joy, peace, and all the other graces that really constitute a Christ-centered, Spirit-filled, happy home.

A Personal Note

These past two chapters contain several suggestions that you read in some of our other books. We hope you will not take offense at this, for we certainly are not trying to be commercial. Our purpose is to help those readers who have a particular problem in an area we have previously covered in detail. What most folks don't realize about our books is that they have grown out of our experiences in counseling people, and each one was addressed to solve a specific problem. It so happens that these are the most common problems facing families today. We are great believers in the power of the Holy Spirit to help people through reading, for we, too, have been helped immeasurably by the writings of others.

We also have great confidence in the power of a single decision. That is, when a man or woman faces the biggest problem area in his life as a sin, that person is well on the road to recovery. In my case, it was anger; in Bev's, it was fear. We hope and pray if you have a problem area that is hindering your family life that the Holy Spirit revealed it while reading this chapter and that you are willing to make the big decision that can revolutionize your life. Face the problem area as sin. Let God cleanse you and remove that habit from your life. Remember the divine promise: "I can do all things through Christ who strengthens me"

(Philippians 4:13). You can have victory over your greatest emotional problem! And the way our Lord strengthens us for that victory is through His Holy Spirit.

The Roles
of the Wife

The supreme hallmark of the Spirit-controlled family is not happiness, well-behaved children, or prosperity. It is obedience to the Word of God. The happiness and fulfillment experienced by the Spirit-controlled family are a result of that obedience. Our Lord said, "Blessed [happy] are those that hear the word of God, and keep it!" (Luke 11:28; see also Psalm 119:1 and John 13:17). The two requirements for happiness are hearing the Word and keeping the Word. Based on those verses, the following formula has been developed:

Hearing the Word of God + **Keeping the Word of God** = **HAPPINESS**

Everyone seeks happiness on a lasting basis. It is never found, however, as the result of a quest, but as a consequence of obedience to God's Word. This is significantly true for the family. For that reason, now that we have reviewed the biblical solution to marriage's six greatest enemies, let us return to the longest New Testament text on the family (Ephesians 5:17–6:4) and examine the three results of the Spirit-controlled life: 1) a song in the heart, 2) a thanksgiving attitude, and 3) a submissive spirit (5:19-21). These results set the stage for a most significant subject: the roles of both wife and husband.

God has carefully outlined the roles of the woman and the roles of the man. Just as they have complementary physical characteristics, so they enjoy complementary roles in marriage. The success of both roles demands cooperation by both partners. That is why He prefaced the role instruction with verse 21: "Submitting to one another in the fear of God." Partners who truly submit to each other have no difficulty teaching on roles or subjecting themselves to them, and thus they help each other fulfill those roles.

The roles of the wife are filled with the challenge to become a versatile woman. More than being a mother, lover, or helpmeet, the success-seeking young woman is assured of a multifaceted career—a challenge that few professions can offer. The circle above establishes the various roles of the wife that we will cover in this chapter.

The Wife as Helpmeet

A "helpmeet" is one who can adequately fulfill the needs of her partner. Ephesians 5:22 instructs women: "Wives, submit to your own husbands, as to the Lord." This does not mean that the woman is inferior or unequal, but that she remains under the authority of the husband. She is a subordinate, a vice president, who serves directly under the head of the household or the president, who is the husband. Because this is God's design, she cannot be a spiritual woman without obeying the command of submission. Verse 22 follows directly from verse 18, which tells her to be filled with the Spirit. The true filling of the Holy Spirit will cause and enable a woman to submit to her husband with a loving and willing heart.

A warning to the modern woman is in order. Do not be confused or misled by the false teaching that has swept our country during the twentieth century. Outspoken feminists proclaimed that a woman should not be subordinate to her husband; she should "do her own thing" and act as a free-thinker, even to the point of changing roles with the man. Such labels as NOW, ERA, or IWY purportedly grant feminist leaders the authority to speak for all American women. However, many of these feminists are not married to happy husbands, some are divorced, others are known lesbians, and few demonstrate the characteristics of "femininity." When speaking out against husbands and families, they are rebels against God. Christian women need to rise up and unanimously declare that the radical feminist protesters represent only themselves. And since much in their platform is not in accord with God's plan for womanhood, it is impossible to follow the entire program and remain Spirit-controlled women.

The Bible teaches women that their attitude toward their husbands should be that of reverence, respect, and submission. "Submission" does not imply that a woman is stripped of her rights, manacled, and reduced to being a slave. On the contrary, submission allows her *more* freedom because she is obeying the law of God and following the path of righteousness. Just as our national freedoms can only be guaranteed as we submit ourselves to the law, so a person can only be truly free when obeying God's principles. The unfortunate women's lib leaders who cry out for more freedom will never experience true liberation until they have first met Jesus Christ and followed His plan for women's freedom.

Submission does not mean suppression or silence; it does not incarcerate a woman in a concentration camp. To be a real helpmeet means to help by offering your thoughts, insights, and feelings. Every wife will have opinions and personal convictions on most subjects, and they may not always agree with her husband's. Submission does not involve closing her mouth, shutting off her brain, and surrendering her individuality.

The loving husband who is wise will seek the insights of his wife before he makes that final decision on issues that affect the family. We have found in our own marriage that we repeatedly see things differently and frequently do not agree on how to approach difficult circumstances. Because Tim has allowed me to develop my own thoughts and feelings, thus retaining my uniqueness, he listens respectfully to my counsel and considers it carefully before making the final decision.

Occasionally, I have unduly influenced him, and he has made an incorrect decision. This has caused me to be more cautious and to weigh my remarks carefully, being certain that they are words of wisdom, for they carry substantial weight with him. I have learned through the years that the Holy Spirit gives special wisdom to husbands who are following the pattern of a Spirit-filled man. When the wife has offered her observations and convictions, she *submits* in committing her husband to God as he makes the final decision. She must submit even more when that decision is contrary to her own perspective. After all, there can only be one authority, one general, one president of the corporation. When the wife entrusts her husband and the decision to God, she is submitting fully and is leaving the consequences, good or bad, to her heavenly Father.

True submission is in force when her attitudes and actions are in complete agreement. It is not a matter of *pretending* to be submissive, for her genuine attitude and desire should be to submit. In addition, she is not subject to her husband because he is such a "wonderful, well-deserving person who dearly loves his wife and is consistently obedient to God." She will not protest, "I will only yield to that carnal man when he straightens out and regains sound spiritual stability." No, she submits because she wants to be obedient to God and maintain a close relationship with Him. The wife's attitudes and actions of submission are a measure or barometer of her relationship to Christ. Verse 22 charges her to be subject to her own husband *as to the Lord.* The next two verses compare the wife/husband relationship to that of the church and Christ. As the church is subject to or under the authority of Christ so should the wife be under the authority of her husband.

Remember, the wife should not submit simply in order to reap results in her husband. Her true obedience lies in submission as his helpmeet, leaving the change and results up to God. One woman asked, "How can I submit to my husband when he isn't obeying what God commanded him to do?" I replied, "Submission is not contingent on the actions of your partner. Leave him to the Holy Spirit."

Another woman rejected the teachings on the authority of the husband. She argued, "Why is so much said about how the woman submits, and so little is required of the husband?" Because of her rebellious attitude toward God, this same woman has had difficulty in totally surrendering to Jesus Christ. She wants to play the game of life *her* way, even though she will lose. You cannot win without playing according to God's rules.

While leading a women's Bible study one day, I was interrupted by a troubled wife who grumbled, "Why is it that the woman gets the most difficult part of the marriage relationship, that of submitting?" Before I could answer, a transformed rebel replied, "I must disagree with you. The husband has the most difficult position. He is responsible for making final decisions that affect the wife, the children, and their future. All I am required to do is submit to him and serve as a helpmeet. The blame or glory for decisions falls wholly on him." That stimulated a very lively discussion, and we concluded that God's assignments to husbands and wives were not in accord with their individual abilities, but rather with their utter dependence upon Him, thus enabling them to fulfill the roles assigned.

In God's eyes their roles are balanced: "Nevertheless, neither is man independent of woman, nor woman independent of man, in the Lord" (1 Corinthians 11:11). The man is the head of the woman, but the woman is the one who gives birth to the man. One cannot function adequately without the other. The wife is told to submit to her own husband as unto the Lord. Why? Because the husband sits in the place of Christ in authority and responsibility. He is the head of the family, the image and glory of God, whereas "the woman is the glory of man" (1 Corinthians 11:7). Neither has a simple assignment, but their roles can be fulfilled when the Holy Spirit is in control of their lives and their greatest desire is to be obedient to God.

Submission is reserved "to your own husband." Women are not expected to be subject to men in general. Some extreme teachings have grown from this biblical injunction, including the false idea that women should be subject to all men, or that single girls should be under the authority of their single male dates. Do not misconstrue the explicit limits of this scriptural command. The wife is to respect and reverence *her own husband*. However, when a single girl is considering marriage, she should definitely ask herself whether this prospective husband is one to whom she could lovingly submit after marriage. Is he the kind of individual she could respect and reverence? Could she willingly place herself under his authority? If not, then marriage would be a great risk.

A wife loves the qualities in her husband that distinguish him from other men. She is attracted to his manhood, and part of that manliness is that he will be the leader of the home. If she refuses to submit and begins to dominate him, she will destroy that part of him that is God-designed and unique: his leadership capability. In subverting this, she is on the road to sacrificing her love and respect for that man. A woman who nags generates one of two responses in her husband: 1) He becomes stubborn, irritable, and obstinate or 2) he gives in just to keep peace, though inside he begins to resent her and harbor bitterness in his heart. Whichever results, he becomes less than the man she envisioned when they married. Eventually, the unique manly characteristics that originally attracted her will fade from view, leaving both partners unfulfilled and unhappy.

Later in marriage the woman who has never learned submission in action and attitude wakes up to another potential problem. During the days of child-raising, she dominated the children and bossed them around. When the children have grown, her increased self-confidence and dominance may then be directed toward the husband. Because her wits and skills have developed over the years, her husband may now serve as the sole target for her domination. The retirement years then become the "rough and rugged years" instead of the "restful and relaxed years." The latter period of life will be what you have been becoming together.

Why a Wife Should Submit to Her Husband

1. *She will never be a Spirit-filled woman unless she submits.* There is no other way to become a godly woman without fulfilling the command to submit to the husband. Any other demonstrations of the Spirit-filled life will be illegitimate. This also applies to strong-willed choleric women. We know such a lady, who all but destroyed her marriage by using her quick wit and forceful personality to run the entire family. She was a very able Bible teacher who one day was brought under conviction while preparing a message on the home from Ephesians 5:18–6:4. Suddenly she realized she was the

leader of her family and that was the real cause of the friction she and her husband were constantly experiencing. All of that changed as she realized she was not really the spiritual woman she claimed to be because she was not submissive to her husband. Surrendered to her Lord, she became obedient to her role in the marriage and today enjoys a relationship with her husband that is a model to all who know them.

2. *She presently has or will ultimately experience an emotional need to lean on a husband.* Her temperament will determine whether she leans on him early in marriage or reaches that point with maturity. The phlegmatic and melancholy temperaments will adjust quite readily to leaning on their husbands in the early days of marriage. They normally shy away from the burden of being independent and find it comfortable to lean on their partner. However, sanguine and choleric women are much more independent and enjoy the role of leadership and responsibility. But even they reach the stage in life when they need to lean on the strength and security of a loving husband. How they have submitted in the early years of marriage will greatly determine how much the husband can be counted on for leaning in the latter years.

3. *Her husband has a need for her to submit.* This is not something the husband learns or tries to develop. It is a built-in need which God designed for him. He greatly needs to be respected and admired, just as she needs to be loved. The husband can become head of the household in two ways. One is by the wife's election. She determines in her heart that this is right and, as she submits, she "elects" him to be the authority of the home. The second way occurs when the husband demands to be the head and becomes a self-appointed dictator. The first choice, resulting from two people willing to be led by the Holy Spirit, will lead to a loving and harmonious relationship. The second choice is

self-motivated and, since it does not give way to the Spirit's leading, it produces friction and resentment. A husband cannot be the loving authority of the wife unless she allows him to be through submission.

4. *Their children need her submission to grow up with normal sex direction and proper role examples.* The child's greatest potential for a happy, normal marriage relationship will be founded upon the example set by Mom and Dad. He can best learn at home how a husband should function as head of the family and the wife as submissive helpmeet.

Submitting to an Unsaved Husband

The questions often arise: "Should a wife submit to an unsaved husband?" and "How far must she go in submission?" Large numbers of Christian women are married to unsaved husbands who have not accepted Jesus Christ as Savior and Lord, so these are important questions to consider.

It is commanded in 1 Peter 3:1: "Likewise you wives, be submissive to your own husbands, that even if some do not obey the word, they, without a word, may be won by the conduct of their wives." Is that a clear answer? "Likewise" refers back to 1 Peter 2:21-25, which establishes that Christ has been an example for us to follow. Even though we strayed like sheep, we have now returned to the Shepherd. You, dear wife, must be an example of Christ, exhibiting behavior and attitudes in the home that will win your husband to Christ. It will not be your words of nagging or preaching that will woo him, but your devoted behavior and your submission. When you put yourself under his authority and demonstrate honor, respect, and loving deeds, Jesus Christ will be seen more clearly in your life than through any words you could ever speak. Nagging and preaching will only drive a wedge between your husband and Jesus Christ.

In some homes more sermons are preached to husbands

than a minister could ever deliver to his congregation. Yet these same dominant, preachy figures at home will come to church and pray publicly for their unsaved husbands. More would be accomplished if they would go home and apologize to their husbands for nagging, place themselves under their husbands' authority, and begin to let their behavior at home speak for itself. Jesus Christ can more beautifully be seen through a changed life than through the greatest oratory in the world. If these women want to win their husbands to Christ, they need to concentrate more on their relationship to Christ and submission to their husbands than on church activities and a busy Christian social life. Their prayer should be; "Lord, change me" prior to, "Lord, save my husband." If the woman's husband is still unsaved, she must confront herself with the thought, "Perhaps he has not been able to see enough of Christ in me."

Submission is the key word. The only exception to this absolute rule is if the husband should ask her to do something that is contrary to the teachings of the Bible, such as stealing or committing adultery. Then he is no longer acting under the authority of God, who never authorizes us to do something that He has previously disallowed. For the Bible teaches that "we ought to obey God rather than men" (Acts 5:29).

The Wife as Home Manager

The husband is to be the supervisor of the home, but the wife will do the actual managing. This does not mean that she will make all the decisions. Rather, she will put into operation the general policies that have already been formulated by the supervisor and the manager together, including the decisions that fall within her sphere.

Norman V. Williams in *The Christian Home* refers to the origins of the two words *husband* and *wife*. The word *husband* means "house-band." He is the one who "bands" or "binds" the home together. The strength and the stability that the band must possess to hold the family together is represented by the husband. In contrast, the word *wife* means "weaver." She is the one who uses her clever hands to weave into the family fabric the beautiful designs which produce much joy and blessing.

Too often women say, "I'm just a homemaker," sensing that they may have missed something in life by following such a calling. That is one reason why we prefer to label her as a "home manager." The challenges are so numerous that the position should be elevated to managerial level. Our standards for home management seem to have dwindled since the example of the "virtuous woman" described in Proverbs 31. There was a day when that woman and I were not on speaking terms. In fact, I used to close my ears at the mere mention of the Proverbs 31 woman. I considered her standards far out of reach and extremely impractical. But today, perhaps after developing maturity and experiencing spiritual growth, I can clearly recognize her sterling example to all Christian women. When her functions are translated into present-day activities, they formulate a practical goal that we can set before ourselves to frame characteristics that we can hope to attain. It certainly takes the "just" out of "just a homemaker." Permit me the privilege of giving Proverbs 31:10-31 a LaHaye paraphrase for the twentieth-century woman:

The Twentieth-Century Woman of Proverbs

Proverbs 31:10—An excellent wife is hard to find. She cannot be bought with expensive jewels or fancy sports cars. Her inner beauty cannot be purchased; it is far greater than money can buy.

31:11—Her husband trusts her with all of his possessions. He is not concerned that she will drain the bank account or run up the charge account for her own whims. Rather, she will help to save and economize in order to establish financial security.

31:12—She is a devoted helpmeet for his good, a responder to his love, and one who lives for his fulfillment.

31:13—She decorates the home, keeps the house tidy, and even mops the floor with a song in her heart and praise on her lips.

31:14—She shops wisely at the local supermarket and fresh-vegetable stands for the best buys in food and provides well-balanced, nutritious meals that are attractively served.

31:15—She rises early in the morning and serves a good breakfast to her husband and children before starting her day's schedule.

31:16—She participates in the "cottage industry" from her own home. From the money she earns, she pays her children's tuition for a Christian education.

31:17—She goes to the local health spa and exercises her body to keep physically fit and strong.

31:18—She senses when her muscles are well-toned, because she can keep up with the busy pace of her family well into the evening.

31:19—She picks up her reading material when she sits down, and keeps her mind busy as she expands her knowledge.

31:20—She makes time to assist those who are needy, making soup and casseroles for sick neighbors and arranging time for volunteer charity work for the poor.

31:21—She is a season ahead, planning what warm winter clothes will be needed for the family before the snow begins to fall.

31:22—She selects her own wardrobe carefully and is well groomed in modest apparel. She is not seen outside her home with curlers in her hair, nor does she dress to gain attention.

31:23—Her husband is a respected businessman among the leaders of the community.

31:24—She volunteers some of her time to the local crisis

pregnancy center. She also atttends the monthly Prayer Action Chapter for Concerned Women for America to pray for her community and her nation.

31:25—Charm and self-confidence are her characteristics, and she faces the future with joy and hope.

31:26—She speaks with wisdom from studying the Word of God, and her life is an example of kindness to others.

31:27—She manages her home with great care and does not sit around idly, watching TV or chatting with her friends on the telephone.

31:28—Her children love and respect her, and her husband sings her praises, saying:

31:29—"You, my darling, are the greatest woman God could have given me."

31:30—A charming and beautiful woman can be deceiving, but a woman who reveres the Lord shall be praised.

31:31—Her children and her community, who know her well, will see all that she has done and will admire and praise her.

Did you catch the theme which runs through every activity of the Proverbs woman? Her career is centered in her home and family. Everything she does is to better her home and improve the family. She is the "weaver" who intertwines the different threads of the home to produce the beautiful finished fabric—her family. What a rewarding career, for in the end they rise up and praise her!

Here are some of a wife's characteristics as a home manager: reflector of inner beauty as developed from walking with God, trustworthy partner, careful budgeter rather than a spendthrift, submissive wife, committed helpmeet, tender lover, cheerful homemaker, tidy housekeeper, interior decorator, purchasing agent, alert manager of her time, creative cook, chauffeur, businesswoman, wise investor of money, physical-fitness expert, maker of hand-stitchery, volunteer worker, compassionate neighbor, wardrobe planner, clothes designer, wife of a busy husband, concerned about the lack or morals in her community and nation, student of the Word, one who daily walks with the Lord, an example of a gracious and godly woman. Her husband has assigned her the management of the home—an area in which to make decisions and sharpen her wits. She certainly need not feel inferior or suppressed. In fact, at times she may feel that it is more than she can handle, or she may look upon it as the exciting challenge in life that she was seeking.

The success of the home manager depends upon her attitude of heart toward the job. There is much room for creative self-improvement in every area of the Proverbs woman's career. Or she can decide that this routine is drudgery and that "I am a prisoner in my own home." The Spirit-filled home manager will develop her capabilities and say in her heart, "Whatsoever you do, do it heartily as unto the Lord."

The Wife as Lover

The Bible does not say much to wives about loving their husbands, yet husbands are commanded several times to love their wives. The woman seems to have an emotional nature that makes it easier for her to love. The husband apparently possesses a one-track mind which can get involved in his business, sports, or other activities, and thus he needs to be reminded to love his wife. She can assist the husband in remembering that he is to love her by being as neat and attractive as possible. Love is not a one-sided affair. It develops out of mutual esteem and admiration for one another.

As that feeling grows, it can be expressed beautifully by the intimacy of the act of marriage. The wife need not be afraid to enjoy this relationship with her husband, for it was designed by God. The Creator saw that it was not good for Adam to be alone, so He created Eve and said that they were to become one flesh. Normally, the woman is a responder to her husband's love, but it is in God's order for her to be the initiator from time to time. According to 1 Corinthians 7:3,4: "Let the husband render to his wife the affection due her, and likewise also the wife to her husband. The wife does not have authority over her own body, but the husband does. And likewise the husband does not have authority over his own body, but the wife does." The next verse charges both spouses: *"Do not* deprive one another. . . ."* Many of us grew up in an era which believed that nice ladies did not admit they enjoyed the act of marriage and certainly would not be aggressive. However, it does not make sense that God would give the wife authority over her husband's body if she was not to enjoy it. No, the wife is meant to fulfill her role as a lover, just as the husband is instructed to love his wife.

Love can be nurtured and developed as a woman learns to participate in the interests of her husband. It helps to know enough of the rules of a football game to share his love for the sport. The wife gains much by learning more about the kind of work he does so she can speak intelligently about it. By building a relationship within his interests, she is also laying a better foundation for their love relationship. After all, there should be more to marriage than just those intimate moments of sex.

A woman can show her love by being more alluring. With all the helps available for ladies today to improve themselves, there is no excuse for her to look like a leftover from a garage sale. A dash of perfume and freshly brushed hair will put a new sparkle in her eye. She can look fresh and clean when she meets him at the door and be ready with a warm kiss that has prospects for the future. A twinkle in her eye and a smile on her face will tell him that she is happy to see him, and if he smells dinner cooking in the background, he will surely know it.

There are other benefits in love besides the pleasure a wife receives from it. When children see Mom and Dad exhibit expressions of love for each other, it helps to build a secure atmosphere around them. On the other hand, when a positive love relationship is missing in the home, the ensuing irritability, quarreling, and criticizing will negatively influence the children's emotional growth and breed insecurity. The best way to provide for your children's future happiness is to raise them in a home where Mom and Dad are lovers.

But what if Mom and Dad have "lost their first love"? It is possible to relearn to love. If the relationship seems dead and the fire needs to be stoked, take heart. Christ can increase your love for your spouse if you sincerely trust Him to do it. In counseling couples who claimed that their love for each other was gone, Tim and I have seen miracles happen. When they genuinely wanted love restored and asked God to help them learn to love all over again, it happened. Along with the prayers, of course, came a change of attitude as well. A tendency toward criticism, nitpicking, complaining, and negativism in general is a real deterrent to love for a partner. Replacing negative attitudes with compliments, approval, and praise will result in a giant step toward becoming lovers.

The Wife as an Ideal of Feminine Beauty

This role is of utmost importance! This is where a woman's real power is hidden. It is sometimes called "the feminine mystique." I am not talking only of her physical feminine beauty, but also the "hidden woman of the heart." A woman's physical beauty will deteriorate and fade with age, but her inner beauty will become more beautiful as she matures in Christ. This inner beauty can come only from walking with God. Our beauty, both inward and outward, should be a testimony of Jesus Christ. The outward appearance should be a manifestation of what is truly in the heart.

Outward Adornment

This subject is a very controversial one, and yet I feel compelled to continue on because it is a misunderstood concept which plays an important role in the life of a woman. If you do not fully agree with me, at least stay with me to the end. I believe every woman has to find God's right answer for her, so I respect what God has led you to do, and hope that you respect God's leading in my life, too.

Discipline Your Body

What difference does outward adornment make? It matters much because a woman's appearance, her grooming, and her size are indications of who controls her life—Jesus Christ or self. Ouch! That sounds harsh, but I am also talking about myself. The times I have let down on my appearance or my weight has jumped have been periods that have been controlled by my own self-indulgence. It was during a time when a lack of self-discipline or self-carelessness or self-pity took over. Accept yourself just as you are and then proceed to ask God to help you change the things that can be changed.

After your next bath, take a good look at yourself in the mirror and commit every roll and bulge to Jesus Christ. Ask for wisdom and discipline into bringing those bulges under control. The same total discipline that causes us to study the Word and have a consistent prayer life will also help us in controlling our weight. I have known some people who had such severe "fat attacks" that they literally had to pray before eating any food. It was not a prayer of thanksgiving, but a prayer which involved presenting one's body to Jesus Christ and asking for control of one's mouth and what was put into it.

Is there any difference between overeating, overdrinking, and oversmoking? The Bible condemns gluttony, drinking, and abuse of our bodies. I have a friend who cannot stop smoking. She has tried every device and plan and has failed in her attempts. I carry a great concern for her because she is a dear friend. She is on my prayer list, and I remember her often. That is all well and good, but on the other hand I have other dear friends who are victims of overstuffing, and I often fail to carry a burden to pray for them. Smoking and excessive eating are equally harmful to the body, and both are considered to be sins. When a woman is Christ-controlled, she will have access to the power that will help her lead a disciplined life that will affect her outward appearance.

Let me leave a note in the minds of the ladies who are naturally trim and have no weight problem. Beware of spiritual pride because you are not overweight. Be patient and pray for your not-so-thin sisters, remembering that you probably have other areas of weakness that they do not have.

Framing the Picture

Our **outward** adorning should not be extreme, nor should it **call** attention to our outer self. There are some people who feel that all cosmetics are wrong; others do not wear any jewelry. Still others wear a good supply of cosmetics plus a variety of rings, earrings, and so on. What is right? "Do not let your beauty be that outward adorning of arranging the hair, of wearing gold, or putting on fine apparel; but let it be the hidden person of the heart, with the incorruptible ornament of a gentle and quiet spirit, which is very precious in the sight of God" (1 Peter 3:3,4). This is not saying that all outward adorning is wrong. However, when it takes priority over the inner adornment, it is sinful. The examples of braiding the hair, wearing gold jewelry, and putting on fine apparel were all very typical practices of the Greeks and the Romans. Much time and effort were put into fancy hairstyles, and women entwined gold jewelry and fancy stones into their hair. The dresses of that day were made from costly silks and brocades. When all of these adornments were given higher priority than the attitude of the heart toward spiritual things, they were wrong.

It is obvious that putting on fine apparel is not wrong, nor is fixing the hair or wearing jewelry; it all depends on what place these practices have in our lives. The verses in 1 Peter speak to us of cutting short some of the time we spend in outer embellishment and putting it into studying the Word of God. The adornment should not be merely external. In other words, it is good to have some external help, but there should be more emphasis put on the hidden woman of the heart. All too often we are guilty of looking only at the outward adornment of others and forgetting the hidden person within. On the other hand, it is possible for the inner beauty to be difficult to see because of the run-down condition of the outer shell. It is highly possible for our outward appearance to resemble a potentially good dinner that is served helter-skelter. All the healthy, delicious ingredients are there to make an excellent meal, but they are just slopped on the plate without order or design. Why not have a proper balance? Let the outward appearance be a frame to surround the picture of the hidden person of the heart. A beautifully framed picture is one that does not draw attention to the frame, but rather the frame aids the viewer in centering attention on the picture itself. And so it is with us. Our frame should not detract from the real person inside. Instead, it should contribute to focusing attention to the real person—the hidden, inner woman.

I am reminded of the biblical Esther who was given one year for self-improvement. God wanted her to be beautiful to fulfill His purpose for her. She checked in at the "Shushan Physical Improvement Spa" and took all the beauty treatments they had to offer. The first six months she was treated with oil of myrrh, and then six months were given to skin care with spices and cosmetics. That is quite a difference from the ten minutes I spend each day, if I can squeeze them in. No wonder Esther won all the beauty contests of her day! But what a woman she was—obedient to God's direction, patient to fit into His time schedule, and courageous to fulfill a difficult role.

There seems to be a growing tendency across our country for young people to have the "natural look." It can be very attractive if done in good taste, but some efforts have gone beyond the natural and have resulted in an unflattering, *unnatural* look. The unkempt, faded, wrinkled and haggard look does not represent the kind of godly person whom the Word uses as an example. In fact, I firmly believe that this kind of appearance is saying to the world that the Christ this person serves is not able to fulfill the promise of Philippians 4:19: "And my God shall supply all your need according to His riches in glory by Christ Jesus." The Proverbs woman is described as wearing beautiful clothes of purple and pure linen, and yet she is described as a truly godly woman who fears and reverences God. Her outward adornment did not take priority over grooming the hidden person of the heart. She dressed appropriately for who she represented—a child of the King.

The Inner Beauty

It is called "the hidden person of the heart" in 1 Peter 3:4. The Bible emphasizes that our priority should be in developing this inner person. It is this quality of the gentle and quiet spirit that is precious in the sight of God. This does not mean that all spiritual women should act like total phlegmatics. On the contrary! God created all of us as unique individuals with varying combinations of the four temperaments. So why would He tell us to be gentle and quiet, when that is a natural characteristic of the phlegmatic? A gentle and quiet spirit is manifested in someone who has learned to be tranquil and constant in the face of all circumstances. The choleric and sanguine are both known to be noisy and explosive. To have a gentle and quiet spirit comes only as a result of working on our attitudes and walking in the Spirit. "You will keep him in perfect peace, whose mind is stayed on You" (Isaiah 26:3).

Here we begin to distinguish where our priorities really are. Most of us have only a limited amount of time for which we can choose what we want to do. Very few women can join the bowling team, take tennis lessons, join a weekly ladies' Bible study, become members of the garden club, lobby their congressman with CWA, and participate in the weekly visitation program of the church all at one time. So we have to pick and choose and sort out our priorities. It may come to the point where there is time for only one extra activity. What will it be? We can rationalize and say, "But I owe it to myself," or "It will make me a more versatile woman," but we must consider what effect each activity has on the hidden woman of the heart and the good of our family. Will it aid in developing a gentle and quiet spirit which is precious in the sight of God?

The beauty in a woman is seen when her life shows forth the fruit of the Spirit. That can only come from walking in fellowship with Jesus Christ: "I say then: Walk in the Spirit, and you shall not fulfill the lust of the flesh" (Galatians 5:16). The woman who walks in the Spirit will portray the fruit of the Spirit: love, joy, peace, patience, kindness, goodness, faithfulness, gentleness, and self-control. Regardless of what her physical features may be like, she will have an inner glow and beauty that shines more brightly than her outward appearance. Her daily walk will be the key to the hidden woman of the heart. If she walks by fulfilling her own desires of the flesh, then her life will demonstrate that. But if she walks in the control of the Holy Spirit, she will live with the fruit of the Spirit in her life. That can only be done by studying the Word of God, fellowshipping with

Him in prayer, and carrying a daily commitment to let God's will be accomplished in her life. It will change her attitudes, actions, and reactions.

This kind of walk does not depend on how gracefully our feet and legs move. On the contrary! A lady can move with all the flowing smoothness of a Paris model and still have a "daily walk" that represents a mangled, crippled inner person. I have known godly women who had a beautiful walk in their daily inner lives, but whose bodies were crippled and deformed. Inner beauty does not depend on a graceful body, but on our intimate, consistent relationship with Jesus Christ.

The Wife as a Mother-Teacher

One young mother told me that she felt as if she were running a seven-day-a-week, 24-hour-a-day preschool or baby-sitting service. When a mother is right in the middle of this period, it seems as if it will never end, and her efforts show no immediate results. It is easy to forget that there are "seasons" in life and the early child-rearing years are for only a season. If she could only stand back and take a look at the overall picture, it would encourage her heart, and she would be more diligent in her efforts. Unfortunately, most mothers cannot do that, so I would like to help them see the picture through my eyes.

Children need mothers for more than receiving life. That is only a small beginning. When that unique little creation arrives on the scene, there is an aura of mystery surrounding him. He has all the features of an adult but in such miniature form. A baby enters the world with much fanfare and expectancy, and yet does nothing to return love to the very woman who gave birth to him. He is totally dependent on outside help and has nothing to give in return. What a challenge to dedication on the part of the mother! The child needs the tender care of a mother who will serve him unselfishly and untiringly without expecting much in return for the first few months of life.

"Children are a heritage from the LORD, the fruit of the womb is His reward" (Psalm 127:3). I can just hear some of you young mothers sigh with disagreement because there are certain times when children appear more like a punishment than a reward. After spending the night walking the floor with a screaming child, or hearing the school principal tell you that your child is failing in all of his subjects, or finding out that your child is heavily into drugs, it is not too hard to understand why some parents feel that their child is a punishment rather than a reward. Yet children are a gift from God, and with the gift He has sent a book of instructions on how to train and prepare that gift for life.

The Complete Instruction Book

One year we gave our sons a Christmas gift of a detailed Erector Set. With that set came a complete book of instructions, and our boys were able to enjoy the gift and create many clever designs because they followed the instructions. Without that help, the gift would have been worthless and a real frustration. Beautiful, complex designs were built because they read the manual carefully and followed what it said. The manufacturer knew what potential the Erector Set held, so he published the instruction book for the benefit and enjoyment of the gift's receiver. The Creator of all children has sent along an instruction book so that His gift might be enjoyed. When the instructions are followed, one can expect to develop the potential and capabilities of a child into a beautiful, complex design with real purpose and reward. Our two sons would read the instructions for the Erector Set and sometimes disagree on how a design should be done. It was important for them to agree on how to do it in order to accomplish the more complex constructions. Likewise, moms and dads need to agree and be united on the "how to" before they can expect many results. The book of Proverbs gives more instruction on raising and training children than any other single book in the Bible. A chapter of this book should be read by parents every day, and Proverbs should be read over and over again.

It is difficult to separate the roles of mother and teacher because so much of the mother's job description turns out to be a teaching responsibility. Ephesians 6 tells the father to be the overseer of the discipline and instruction of the children. But the mother, as the helpmeet, must share in this project and carry out the standards that have been agreed upon. The mother often spends more waking hours with the child than the father, so it is essential that they work together as a team.

Parents United

Probably some of our most heartbreaking counseling sessions have been when mothers and fathers have failed to be united on the teaching and discipline of their children. When the years began to reveal that their divided spirits have produced havoc and despair, they came to us with troubled hearts about their rebellious children. Young parents would avoid some of these traumatic problems if they would agree to be united in disciplining their children at an early age. Children catch on very young when Mom and Dad do not agree, and they begin to play one parent against the other. How much more effective rules and regulations would be if both parents would stand firmly united.

A simple formula which I proposed in *How to Develop Your Child's Temperament* can be put to good use by all mothers:

Instruction + Love + Insistence = Effective Training

It requires all three of these ingredients to have effective training. If any two are used without the third, the training will be inadequate.

The joy of training comes when you begin to see results happening. It may take months and years, but be diligent and "[do] not grow weary while doing good" (Galatians 6:9) because the day will come when you can put away your role of teacher and serve as counselor and enjoy the rewards of the gift. If you give up too early, you will live under the regret that you should have stuck with it and your children would have been different.

None of us is perfect. We look back over our years of parenthood and realize we made a lot of mistakes. But somehow we had the direction from our heavenly Father that our children would be reluctant in obeying Jesus Christ if they did not first learn to obey their parents. We are thankful today that this strong principle of obedience covers over many of the mistakes we made. Our four children have all made professions of faith in Christ and know the importance of walking with the Lord. It is not because they had such good examples from their mother and father, but because they were raised on biblical principles right out of the "complete instruction book."

Chapter 7

The Husband as Leader, Lover, and Provider

$\mathcal{I}$t is not easy to be a good husband. But it is difficult to be good at anything from marriage to sports to scholarship. If you're going to do something, you might as well become as proficient as you can. Fortunately, we Christians are not like the secular sophisticates of our time, who reject all basic guidelines to life and maintain that each generation must find for itself the best way to live. If the automotive industry operated that way, we would still be immersed in the Model T stage. Doubtless, that is the reason for so much unhappiness in the average family—its members are always stumbling around, trying to find the right way to operate.

The Spirit-controlled family is attentive to God's manual on human behavior, the Bible, which gives explicit instructions as to how the family should function. The next diagram shows the variety of roles God planned for the husband. His contribution to family happiness will be determined by how well he assumes each of these roles.

The Husband as Family Leader

God's first assignment for the husband is to be the leader

of his family. Our text in Ephesians 5:23 clearly states, "For the husband is head of the wife, as also Christ is head of the church; and He is the Savior of the body." This accords with Genesis 3:16, where God says to the woman: "Your desire shall be for your husband, and he shall rule over you." This principle is repeated in 1 Corinthians 11:3: "But I want you to know that the head of every man is Christ, the head of woman is man."

Before any young man takes a bride from the protective custody of her father's home, he had better be ready to assume her leadership. It matters not that she is a quick-acting choleric and he a passive phlegmatic—she needs a leader. The most frustrated women today are those who interpret the advice of the women's lib movement as a call to dominate their husbands. In the "book of beginnings" (Genesis), where God laid out the tracks of life for people to run on, He said that a woman's desire shall be to her husband. That is, her basic psychic mechanism is to be a follower of that man who opens his life, home, and possessions to her. Once she marries such a man, her natural inclination is to follow him. If he shirks the role of leadership out of neglect, ignorance (because he did not see such a role exemplified by his father or does not know the Bible), or personal weakness, he is condemning his wife to a lifetime of psychic frustration. Such women gradually become carnal, dominating, neurotic, and obnoxious as the years roll by. It is very difficult for a woman to submit to a man who refuses to lead. A young man best serves God, his wife, and himself when he starts immediately to assume the role of leader in his home. There are plenty of opportunities for the strong-willed wife to use her choleric tendencies, but being the leader of her home is not one of them!

Respect is not innate, as is love. It must be earned, and all husbands should remember that. If your children do not respect you as the head of the home, your entire family is in trouble. I have seen children who loved their father, but felt sorry for him because he was not exercising leadership in their home. One such daughter at 24, a physical education instructor in the public schools and a tennis star, could not relate to her husband, for she was bound up with hate and bitterness toward her mother. Finally the story came out. Her dad was a generous, kindly baker who receded into a shell and succumbed to his wife's intense domination. Clenching her teeth, the daughter growled, "My greatest desire in high school was that just once my daddy would double up his fist and belt my mother in the mouth." Anything short of male leadership in the home has a disastrous effect on the other members of the family.

Whenever we speak of male leadership in the home, we tend to equate it with the old European paternalistic family where the father was a virtual dictator. Such a role, though still common in many homes in northeastern Europe, does not coincide with biblical teaching. God's leadership standard is *always* set before us in love, as we shall see later in this chapter. The husband is to serve as leader of the wife *as Christ is the head of the church.* That constitutes a leadership of love. Our Lord directs us, leads us, makes decisions for us, and takes responsibility for us in a spirit of love and consideration, always maintaining a supreme interest in our good.

The difference between male leadership in the home and *loving* male leadership is that when the husband is forced to make a decision that counters the desires of his wife and children, he must exercise his prerogative in love. "How can the family be assured of that?" you may ask. Very simply: by asking, In whose best interest is the decision being made? The husband's? We have already seen that selfishness has no place in the Spirit-filled home. A loving leader will always make his final decision for the good of the family. Since he is human, he may not always be right, but his motivation should always be directed toward the good of all.

The husband's role of leadership is much like that of the president of a corporation. Many employees work under such a man, some of whom (like his wife) are his equals, and some his superiors—at least intellectually. Andrew Carnegie used to boast that his success could not be attributed to his skills alone, but to the fact that he hired subordinates who were more capable than he. Would such an administrator dictate over superior people? Never. To gain their greatest productivity, he will allow them as much freedom as possible within the corporate structure, always considering their thoughts and opinions when making decisions. Similarly, a wise husband will consider the feelings and ideas of the wife and the children (as the latter mature). Many times he will concur with their arguments, but that does not in one degree lessen his leadership. On occasion, however, he may reject their input and render an unpopular verdict. I would offer five considerations in such a case:

1. Never make a decision without hearing and evaluating your wife's views.

2. Always pray for the decision-making wisdom which God promises to provide (James 1:5).

3. Always check your motivation. Is it really for the family's good, or could it be inspired by selfishness or prejudice?

4. Use tact in effecting your decision. A sensitive father will not alienate the family he loves.

5. Once the decision is made, do not give in under pressure (pouting, temper, frigidity, or any other manifestations of carnality). However, always be open to further evidence that might render your decision obsolete and warrant a change. In the plan of God, the husband should make the final decisions.

Leadership is not an easy role to maintain. At times, during the aftermath of a decision, the leader can get mighty lonely. To be honest, I don't always like making family decisions, but that's part of my job—and husbands, it's yours, too. God holds you accountable as the corporate head of your home. Be fair, be reasonable, be loving, but by all means be a leader.

Decision-making becomes more complex as the family grows. As seen in the next diagram, the mother who functions as a manager, working more closely with the children and the home than does the father, is apt to make decisions primarily from that perspective. The father has to evaluate her suggestions, but from a broader perspective. It is a wise wife who tries to understand her husband's decision if they can't afford a vacation, new clothes for the children, or a new item of furniture. He may be thinking ahead about a

GOD'S LINES OF AUTHORITY

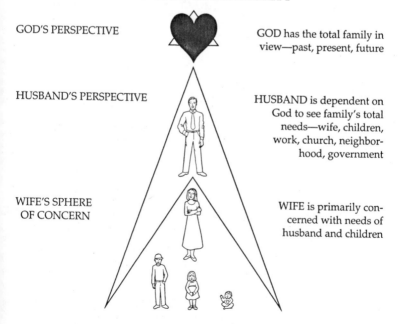

GOD'S PERSPECTIVE

GOD has the total family in view—past, present, future

HUSBAND'S PERSPECTIVE

HUSBAND is dependent on God to see family's total needs—wife, children, work, church, neighborhood, government

WIFE'S SPHERE OF CONCERN

WIFE is primarily concerned with needs of husband and children possible layoff, taxes, or house repairs. One of the most difficult areas of interpersonal relationships arises when we attempt to see life through the eyes of another person. Ideally, in spite of temperament differences, couples should see things alike as their love matures.

Note to Husbands—the Other Side of Submission

Before passing from this subject, two brief notes to husbands are in order. The first concerns submission from the woman's perspective. It is not easy for a strong-willed woman to submit to a man "in everything." Even a Spirit-filled choleric wife will have to learn that role. You can help as a husband by being fair in carefully attending to her point of view and even accepting it whenever possible without relinquishing your role as leader. If you are predominantly melancholy and your wife is choleric, don't be surprised if many of her suggestions are more practical than yours. The wise husband is man enough to admit that quite often her ideas are better than his.

In our case, Bev usually takes longer to make a decision than I, but when she eventually makes up her mind, her judgment is often best. I learned years ago that she will not be pressured into quick decisions. In fact, she will invariably throw ice water on anything suddenly thrust upon her. In our early, selfish days, that became a bone of contention, for when I evaluated a proposal and pressed my decision upon her, she would balk but I would force her to go along with me. Oh, she didn't scream and holler. Phlegmatics don't do that. But she was superb at clamming up and dragging her feet. I thoroughly enjoyed my role as "enforcer," but my Gestapo tactics did nothing for our marriage. Now I have learned to spring nothing on her quickly. Instead, in love, I plan long-range and give her plenty of lead time. In fact, a good approach is: "Honey, I've got an idea; don't give me a decision now, but think it over." Then

I share the plan and back off for a few days. About 85 percent of the time she agrees with me or improves on my idea by the time we discuss it again. The other 15 percent of the time we either abandon the idea or she goes along joyfully, now that she too is filled with the Spirit.

The point is to go out of your way to adapt your leadership to the temperament and personhood needs of your wife. Her agreement and submission do not have to come at the expense of her self-respect if you will let her express herself and then demonstrate that you value her opinion. For instance, never forget that she is a far greater authority on the needs of your children than you are. She has spent ten times as many hours with them by their fifth birthday than you have, and consequently knows them better. I wish every husband could sit in the counseling room and hear a well-educated, intelligent, and loving wife exclaim, "The most maddening thing about my husband is his refusal to listen to my side of the argument." Wives don't want agreement as much as they want a platform to air their views.

A couple we were very close to several years ago provides a tragic illustration. He had a dominant, compulsive choleric melancholy temperament with a brilliant mind and an insufferable determination to be right all the time. His wife was also a strong-willed woman, but no match for him. He had to be right (and obeyed) in everything, from how she cooked to how she kept house. Needless to say, she did not have a happy life—and neither did he. Their love died long before the marriage did. That turned what could have been an ideal life into a living nightmare. I tried to counsel them several times, but finally he turned against me, the church, and many of his Christian friends. Suddenly his wife became violently ill. That changed him. He couldn't do enough for her in an attempt to reach out to help her, but all he could do was spend money on doctors. Finally, she died a painful death. At her funeral he wept bitter tears through which he repeatedly said, "If only I had our lives to live over again, I would have treated her differently." What he meant by that is treat her with love, respect, and dignity. In his case that would have meant listening to her instead of jumping to conclusions, and speaking kindly instead of always criticizing her. Unfortunately, with death there is no second chance. There is just remorse, and sometimes it lasts a lifetime. Most men would treat their wives and families differently if they really understood what their wives wanted.

We could all learn from the results of an international survey taken by the League of Large Families in Brussels (cited in *The Seven Stumbling Blocks Ahead of Husbands*, a publication of The American Institute of Family Relations), indicating the seven most common failings of husbands, in the opinions of wives:

1. A lack of tenderness
2. A lack of politeness
3. A lack of sociability
4. A failure to understand the wife's temperament and peculiarities
5. Unfairness in financial matters
6. Frequency of snide remarks and sneers at the wife before company or the children
7. A lack of plain honesty and truthfulness

It has been my observation that Christian wives would add one more important failing to that list. For at the question time during my 900 Family Life Seminars, one of the most frequent questions is, "How can I get my husband to become the spiritual leader of our home?" We will answer that in the rest of this and in the next chapter.

Handling Spirit-Filled Disagreements

Even two people filled with the Spirit will not experience

total agreement on everything. If that were a requirement, Bev and I would be disqualified, for we see everything differently. I like to work furiously right up to departure time for a vacation, pack the car, then as I'm backing out of the driveway prior to a 3000-mile trip ask, "Would you look in the glove compartment and see if you can find a map?" Bev is the type who contacts the automobile club two months in advance to plan a basic strategy for the trip. That difference shows itself in all our decisions, from breakfast cereal to wallpaper. We are more surprised when we agree than when we disagree.

Soon after being filled with the Spirit, we developed a very simple procedure that has helped resolve those contrary choices. Whenever it is "comfortable" to do so, one of us agrees with the other (about 40 percent of the time each of us "gives in"). The remaining 60 percent of our disagreements are settled by agreeing to "pray about it." God has promised to give His children wisdom when they ask, and we have found that He really does. He will cause one of us to acquiesce joyfully with the other's point of view, or many times He will lead us to an entirely different decision. The number of times I am forced to make a final decision which is unpleasant to Bev thus becomes infrequent.

Being a Good Leader

The second note on submission from a woman's viewpoint is that it is easier for her to respect a man who will stand up and be a good leader. All temperaments possess a natural weakness in leadership which must be strengthened. Cholerics are strong, aggressive leaders who need to develop compassion and consideration for others. Sanguines are prone to be inconsistent leaders, quick to make impossible decisions which they expect the wife to execute. They need to make fewer but more deliberate decisions and implement them graciously. Melancholies tend to be legalistic nitpickers who would return the family toward Old Testament or pharisaical rules and even then find something to criticize. They need to be leaders known for their "sweet reasonableness." The phlegmatic needs to work on being a more aggressive leader. He prefers to head for a garage after work and putter around his workbench, abdicating his leadership role to the wife at a time when his teenagers are making life-molding decisions and evaluations.

A missionary wife came to us in tears after our seminar in their base city in Asia, saying, "I am losing all respect for my husband. He leaves all the discipline of our three teenage children to me." This man, interestingly enough, was a very effective missionary. But strong home leadership was difficult for him, so rather than trust the Holy Spirit for the self-control and goodness He promises, he was reaping a lifetime of relinquished leadership at a desperate period in his teenagers' lives.

A case in point that she shared was his treatment of their TV viewing—one of the biggest bones of contention in most Christian homes if the problem is not solved before the children reach five years of age. As the moral standards of TV entertainment (*corruption* is a better word) were plunging to all-time lows, he took strong exception to the immoral programs his children watched, but left the execution of his standards to his wife. If he came home and found them watching something he disapproved of, he would run to her and complain, "You're letting the children watch one of those programs I have forbidden." When she responded, "Well, you tell them to shut it off," he would reply, "That's your job." Thus the spiritual head of the family abrogated his role and played second-string to his wife, even though God has given men a deeper register of voice and a masculine, commanding bearing that makes discipline of the older children much easier for them than for their wives. I found under similar circumstances that the situation merely required me to effect the lowest commanding voice I could muster and say, "Kids, do you want to turn that program off or do you want me to?" That was the signal which opened two options: 1) They turned the channel to a more acceptable program, or 2) I turned the TV off altogether.

Love and respect run on the same street: One will not endure long without the other. To keep your wife's love you must earn her respect—and believe me, you need her respect!

The Husband as Ideal Lover

After God, the greatest love in a man's life should be his wife. He is commanded to love her more than he loves his neighbor, for Ephesians 5:25 states he is to love her as Christ loved the church. He is told only to love his neighbor "as himself." The Greek work for *love* here is the same used in John 3:16 and other passages to describe God's love for man in sacrificing His Son. For that reason, we say a man should love his wife sacrificially.

The late Dr. Harry Ironside, my favorite Bible teacher, once told of a young husband who came to him wondering if he loved his wife so much that it interfered with his love for the Lord. The lad said she was the center of his first thought in the morning, the last at night. He would call her several times a day. Even when he prayed, he couldn't get her out of his mind. Wise old Dr. Ironside asked, "Young man, do you love her enough to die for her?" After hesitating for a moment, the husband replied, "No, I guess not," to which the aged counselor responded, "Your problem is, you don't love her enough!"

No emotion is more needed, more talked about, and less understood than love. Poems by the reams have been written about it; stories, plays, and movies have portrayed it; mankind never tires of hearing about it. Yet except for mother-love, the reality of love's expression is seldom experienced. True husband-love is supernatural, a result of being filled with the fruit of the Spirit. That kind of love is a treasure that grows and matures through the years, not depending on any single event but requiring a lifetime to express. As the result of a man and woman sharing their total selves unconditionally, it can absorb conflict, disagreement, disappointment, tragedy, and even selfishness. True love is not dependent on two perfect persons, but on two people filled with the Spirit of God. Love is the ideal way to face the unknown and potentially bumpy road to the future. It is to marriage what shock absorbers are to a car—love cushions the rough spots in life. A husband who nurtures a love like that is guaranteed a steady return on his investment (Galatians 6:7,8). It is well worth a lifetime of cultivation.

Test Your Love

Through the years we have been asked to develop a test that would basically reveal a husband's love for his wife. The following questions are quite revealing. You may score yourself 0 to 10 on each of them. Read the questions carefully and try to be objective.

1. Do you have a strong and affectionate bond of caring about your wife's needs and desires that inspires a willingness on your part to sacrifice to fulfill them?

2. Do you enjoy her personality, companionship, and friendship?

3. Do you share common goals and interests which you communicate about freely?

4. Do you respect and admire her in spite of recognized needs or weaknesses in her life?

5. Do you have sexual attraction for each other that leads frequently to a mutually satisfactory expression of the act of marriage?

6. Do you desire children (if physically possible) who share both of your physical and

temperament characteristics and to whom you can impart your moral and spiritual values?

7. Do you have a vital faith in God that is a helpful influence on her spiritual life?

8. Do you have a sense of permanence and possession about her such that other women are not in like manner attractive to you?

9. Do you have a growing desire to be with her?

10. Do you have a genuine appreciation for your wife's successes?

Total Score _____

If you scored 90 to 100, you are doing well. If in the 80s, you need to work on your love. A score in the 70s suggests that your deficiencies are getting serious, and below 70 indicates that you need help soon (you should not only "walk in the Spirit," but you should also consult your pastor).

What Is Love?

Everyone agrees that love is a feeling. Where it comes from or how one gets it inspires a variety of answers. As a feeling, love is a motivator that causes action, and for that reason the best way to define love is to examine what it does. The diagram on page 138, based on 1 Corinthians 13:4-8, particularly applies to a husband's love for his wife, for it describes the way he will treat her when he is controlled by the Holy Spirit. In fact, inadequacy in any of these nine expressions of love is a sure indication that he is more filled with himself and his own spirit than with the sacrificial love imparted by the Holy Spirit.

Love heart. True love is patient or enduring, as the Greek word really indicates. Most translators label this word

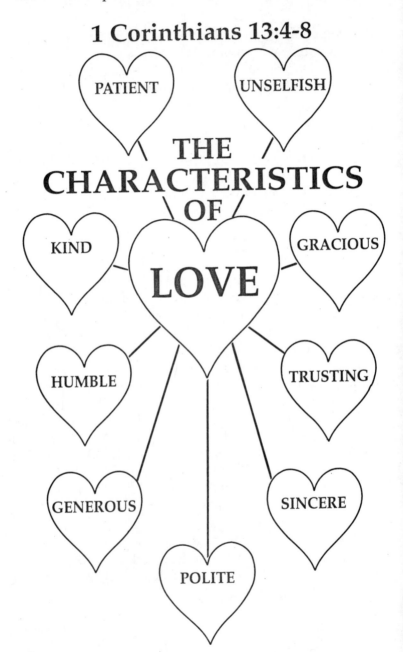

1 Corinthians 13:4-8

PATIENT

UNSELFISH

THE
CHARACTERISTICS
OF

KIND

LOVE

GRACIOUS

HUMBLE

TRUSTING

GENEROUS

POLITE

SINCERE

"longsuffering." That is, it will accept slights and rebuffs lovingly or without retaliation. A good test of this is how you respond during your wife's menstrual period. She needs extra love and tender warmth at a time when she may be less lovable. It is a wise husband who anticipates that time of the month or any of his wife's other pressure points and goes out of his way to show his love regardless of her attitude.

One husband said, "I love my wife, but I get so impatient with her sometimes. What's wrong?" I answered, "Your problem is that you love yourself at those impatient times more than you love your wife. Otherwise you would be patient."

Henry Drummond said years ago, "Love understands and therefore waits." Bill Gothard today observes, "Lust cannot wait to get; love cannot wait to give."

Kind heart. To a woman, the king of all expressions of love is kindness. Women are stronger emotionally than we think. A woman can suffer hurt, offense, and pain far better than a man but in the home she is particularly vulnerable to unkindness from her husband or children. That is especially true of words. Most men do not realize that just as they are visually stimulated, their wives are verbally responsive. The man who comes home from work and barks out criticism, demands, and insults is not only exhibiting carnality but is also committing sexual suicide. The lover who walks in at night filled with love, joy, and peace will resort to kind words and tender speech. He is motivated purely by love and respect for his wife, but his behavior is in fact preparing them both to culminate their many expressions of love in the act of marriage sometime during the evening. Love is its own reward.

Love expresses itself in many kind ways—gifts, flowers, unexpected remembrances—and a host of thoughtful gestures that are meaningful to a wife. All wives do not have the same temperament, so what turns one woman on may be meaningless to another. Find out what your wife likes and responds to, then express your love tangibly.

My wife, for example, prefers flowers. Personally, I think they are a waste! If I had my way, we would arrange plastic flowers in our home, for they require no watering, pruning, or care, yet they always look nice There is just one thing wrong with that idea: Bev hates plastic flowers. Consequently, I still buy flowers from the kid on the corner, just to lighten her day. During the five years I shared with other speakers at seminars, I would always stop on Saturday nights at the flower counter at the San Diego Airport and bring home a bouquet of yellow roses. They did nothing for me, but they sure turned Bev on, and that's what counts. I know you're running out of ideas for gifts. So am I! After more than 40 birthdays, Christmases, anniversaries, Valentine's Days, "sweetest days," and other miscellaneous events, my creativity has been shredded. But kindness keeps us faithful, and it's the thought that counts.

When I put the hand of our daughter Linda into the hand of "Murph" and "gave her away," I had an opportunity that only we preacher fathers enjoy: I performed the wedding ceremony. Looking into that young man's eyes, I was rather startled at how young he looked. The full reality of the moment gripped me. I was entrusting the first treasure of our home, the product of 20 years of love, into his inexperienced hands. (Naturally, I forgot that Bev's dad had done the same to me years before.) Speaking for fathers everywhere, I said to my new son, "Murph, Linda's mom and I don't ask that you make her rich or famous, but we do make one special request as you take her from our home: Always be kind to her." Now, 25 years later, I thank God that he has honored that charge faithfully and has demonstrated that love by always being kind to her. In response, he enjoys her undying love.

Generous heart. True love is so generous that it takes genuine delight in the successes of one's partner. A man in our church can't so much as sing in the shower, but his wife has a beautiful voice. I like to watch him when she sings, for the expression on his face testifies that no one in the church gets more enjoyment from her gift than he does. Contrast that to the man who is so immature that he has forbidden his wife to sing in the choir because he would rather have her sit with him in church. She is being submissive, of course, but not to a loving and sensitive husband. Generous love will spill over into the way a couple spends money, entertains, invests in charitable projects, or in other ways utilizes their resources. Love is giving! The best way to get love is to give it away.

Humble heart. Pride is the greatest single enemy which man faces in life. In 1 Peter 5 Satan is pictured as a roaring lion, seeking to devour man through pride. A proud spirit is a destroyer of true love, and therefore has no place in the life of a Spirit-controlled husband, whose love inspires him to forget himself and his "rights" in deference to the emotional and material needs of the family I am never impressed with the husband whose garage is filled with the latest power tools or whose closet is bursting with the best sporting gear, but whose wife is still limited in the kitchen to hand-me-down utensils.

Polite heart. Electronic door openers and other mechanical contrivances, together with the self-sufficiency tone of our times, do nothing to cultivate courtesy and polite behavior. I have been appalled throughout my travels around the world to see how men have neglected good manners. Many a man no longer opens doors for his wife or remembers which side of the sidewalk on which to escort her. Women, of course, are quite capable of opening doors for themselves, but men need to cultivate these gestures of respect. Women of all ages enjoy being treated as someone special.

I have probably opened 25,000 doors for the special women in my life (Bev and our three daughters), and I anticipate another 25,000 before the friendly undertaker lays me to rest. I not only enjoy treating them like ladies, but I also am gratified by the sense of self-worth such actions engender in a woman. One of our daughters dated a Christian young man of whom we didn't fully approve. He met all of our basic conditions for dating, but there was something crude about him that just didn't inspire me. One date was all it took for our teenager to come home and announce, "Ugh! That's the last time I'm going out with that clod! He doesn't even know how to treat a girl." A few years later, when she wrote to tell us about the lad she met in a Christian college, she attached the following P.S.: "Dad, you'll like him; he treats me like a real lady."

If Jesus Christ, the embodiment of love, were here on earth today, He would treat all women as ladies. We husbands can hardly do less for those lovely creatures who bear our names.

Unselfish heart. We have already observed how selfishness is a matrimonial destroyer. Love, we hasten to add, will erase selfishness and self-seeking. Spirit-controlled love will look for ways to express itself. Every couple has different tastes that usually do not reveal themselves until after marriage. I am a sports nut, and my wife is a lover of culture. To her credit, Bev has, in love, cultivated a genuine interest in athletics. For years we held season tickets to the San Diego Charger games and occasionally have attended basketball, baseball, and hockey events. Although I love her dearly, I cannot honestly share her enthusiasm for opera or the symphony. Oh, I take her on occasion (even though it leaves me a little numb), but very truthfully my basic enjoyment in attending comes from viewing the obvious pleasure it instills in her. You should have seen her the night I took her to hear the Boston Philharmonic Symphony

Orchestra play Tchaikovsky's *Fifth Symphony in E Minor*. I won't tell you how I felt (it wasn't a total loss, however; I designed a chart on the book of Revelation with special emphasis on the tribulation period), but she loved it!

Gracious heart. The best-tempered homes, as we have already seen, will be Spirit-controlled homes. The usual disharmony, short temper, and irritability will be replaced by the gracious love and peace of the Holy Spirit. Such love is not touchy, easily offended, or defensive, and it never responds in anger or hostility, either verbally or emotionally.

Trusting heart. Jealousy is a cruel taskmaster and an unnecessary bedfellow in a Spirit-controlled marriage. Usually it is generated by the insecurities of one partner more than by the deeds of the other. Many couples return from parties or group activities in the midst of violent quarrels because the flirtations or provocations of one partner have fanned the jealousies of the other. True love is trusting and "thinks no evil." If you have a temperament that is easily given to such thoughts, always evaluate the situation through the magnifying glass of love. A loving spirit not only goes the extra mile, but is also quick to excuse. Self-love is quick to condemn.

Sincere heart. Deceit is harmful to any relationship between people, but it is devastating in a marriage. Some of the most heartrending cases I know have involved women who said, "I cannot trust my husband." The tragedy of deceit lies in its principal quality: It never remains static. The man who tells his wife "little white lies" soon starts to feed her "gray" and, ultimately, "big black" lies. Some wives cannot trust their husbands in any area—financially, morally, and so on. I can verify that the immoral man cannot be trusted in anything. Sexual sins lead to lying, financial manipulations, and widespread deceit. Finally, the culprit weaves such a web for himself that he is caught in it and exposed.

True love not only is sincere but also goes out of its way to be honest in word and deed. This is never more apparent than after an argument. When the husband gradually comes to the painful conclusion that he was either wrong or reacted improperly and that he owes his wife an apology, what should he do? I have never found it easy to admit that I acted unreasonably or made an erroneous decision. The male ego seems to assert itself at that moment and declare, "Serves her right! That one will make up for all the times *she* was wrong." But love doesn't keep accounts or play one-upmanship. Instead, it hurries to the aid of the love object and tries to rectify all misunderstandings. The Spirit-controlled husband will quickly confess his error not only to God but also to his partner or his children, as the occasion demands. God in His grace has granted us a merciful way of removing sins and injuries through sincere confession. Many a relationship has been spared needless pain by the simple but manly admission, "Honey, I was wrong, and I hope you will forgive me. I'm sorry I hurt you."

Love Never Fails

Love is a living entity that needs food, water, and cultivation. But even then there are seasons when love rises and falls—particularly in the early stages. Recently I pulled an absolutely brilliant stunt in my backyard. Deciding that the slopes of several banks in our yard were too thinly planted, I bought three large bags of fertilizer and spread them on profusely. In two weeks' time our banks were green and growing. But to my amazement, in six weeks I had the heaviest growth of thick green weeds in Southern California! It was the dormant season for my plants. All I had done was fertilize the weeds that grow at that time of the year. Had I waited two or three months, the plants would have outgrown most of the weeds.

You will find that the intensity of love will rise and fall, depending on the season of life, your spiritual condition, and the priority you attach to your relationship in the light of your vocational and outside pressures. In a survey taken for *Parade* magazine, the average successful business executive indicated he had intercourse with his wife only once a week (only 20 percent said they were carrying on extracurricular activity). According to surveys taken of couples from all walks of life, the average is about 2.5 occasions per week. In a survey taken among 1700 Christian couples for our book *The Act of Marriage*, we found an incidence of almost three times a week. Now what does that suggest to you?

I think we can safely assume that heavy business pressures or stress on a man's mind decrease his interest in lovemaking. In fact, surveys suggest that the more cerebral a man's job, the less frequent is his sexual desire. Those with the greatest desire are men with physical jobs or tasks most easily left at the place of employment when going home at the end of the day. The point is that both men and women will find seasons when their love lives (an expression of their love) will be less than intense. A pastor with three sermons on Sunday morning and one or two on Sunday evening may function as a zero on Saturday nights. Salesmen in the midst of a campaign, professional men driving hard to finish a project, and wives during a time of illness or just before the annual visit of the in-laws probably go through a dormant time. It is perfectly natural so long as it is not protracted. At such times, a good principle to keep in mind appears in verse 8 of 1 Corinthians 13: "Love never fails."

How to Ignite Sputtering Love

"I don't love my wife anymore" is not an unfamiliar wail even to Christian counselors. Most men who make this admission think that they are the first victims of this tragic malady. Unfortunately, it is becoming increasingly common.

Under the pressure of emotional stress in their marriage I have heard men declare, "We never should have been married in the first place! If I hadn't gotten her into trouble, I would never have married her." As a counselor, I find such an attitude an exciting challenge if the person is a Christian. (If not, and the person refuses to receive Christ, I frankly do not know how to help him.) Several years ago I developed the following three steps which will ignite the most sputtering love.

1. *Walk in the Spirit.* Marriage is not a two-way relationship flowing between man and woman. It is a three-way relationship. As we walk in the Spirit, God gives us a love for each other which will flow spontaneously. A breakdown in our relationship as partners will inevitably entail a breakdown in our relationship with God. In fact, Bev and I have used a collapse between us as a signal that we were not walking in the Spirit. By confessing that sin to God, we opened our eyes to the problem.

2. *Never dwell on insults, injuries, hurts, or the weaknesses of your partner.* Every person I have counseled for "lack of love" had developed a well-rehearsed list of grievances to quickly impose upon his or her partner. This noxious response is similar to taking the lid off a septic tank, with all the poisons and stench of the past foaming out. If that sounds extreme to you, it is only because you have not heard the vile things people can think up about their partners. The Bible says, "As [a man] thinks in his heart, so is he" (Proverbs 23:7). The mouth becomes the potent revealer of thoughts. Evil, negative thoughts (even when true) are destructive of good feelings, and thus the Spirit-controlled Christian will not permit evil thoughts to clutter his mind and clog his feelings.

3. *Thank God for ten things about your partner twice daily for three weeks.* We have already noted that the Spirit-controlled

Christian will consistently fulfill the mandate: "In everything give thanks." Constant griping corrupts good emotions, whereas thanksgiving cultivates them. I defy any man to make a list of ten qualities he likes about his wife, thank God each morning and every evening for them, and still have trouble loving her. (I also defy any man to gripe continually about his wife in his mind and still maintain love for her.) The battle for love is won or lost in the mind, not in the heart. Quite clearly, the heart is the servant of what the mind thinks.

The best illustration of this technique occurred several years ago when a friend confessed, "I don't love my wife anymore. In fact, we haven't slept in the same bedroom for three months." Together we scratched out, on a three-by-five card, ten things about her that he liked. He promised to review his list thankfully each morning during his quiet time and each evening during his 35-minute ride home from work. In ten days he enthusiastically exclaimed, "We're back in the same bedroom!" In three weeks he added, "I love that woman more now than in all the years of our marriage." When I asked him if he had memorized his list, he smiled and replied, "Oh, sure, I had that list memorized the third day, so I turned the card over and wrote down 15 more things I like about her." Love begets love, and hateful thoughts beget hate, bitterness, and selfishness.

No man can daily thank God for ten things about his wife without propagating love. You can imagine what love would be engendered if he increased his list to 25 items. Several years have passed, and my friend and his wife remain closer for the most part, but a few months ago he sadly commented at lunch, "We're not sleeping together again!" I asked if he had lost his thanksgiving list, to which he replied, "I knew you were going to ask that!" Together we made another list in spite of his reluctance to "try that again," but it worked in just two weeks. Praise and thanksgiving are powerful factors for igniting love.

Husband: Why You?

Husbands may well ask, "Why does God command me four times to love my wife and only once direct her to love me?" That is a question I have pondered for many years and can offer two possible answers. First, women have a greater need to be loved. As one woman said, "Without love I have no life!" Second, men have a harder time loving Because of their nature, women possess an enormous capacity for love, whereas men have to cultivate theirs. That is why a man should be very careful to walk in the control of the Spirit. He needs the supernatural love of God to be the lifetime lover that God commands him to be and that his wife naively expected him to be when she agreed to become his wife.

As a student of family living for many years, I have come to the conclusion that the man sets the love tone for his home. Women are basically responders to the treatment they are given. So far I have never seen a woman leave a man who is good to her, nor have I been asked to counsel a man who consistently cared for his wife. His expressions of love need not be costly, but they do need to represent that love honestly. While still a very young minister, one Friday night I was called into a wealthy home where the people had everything money could buy but shared no love. The next morning I visited the poorest family in our church to pray for their son who was about to leave for the army. Their home was so sparsely furnished that they had me sit at the end of their breakfast table on the edge of an orange crate. As we prayed, I was impressed with the love in this family, beginning with the father, whose wages were so low that the only thing he had to give his family was his love. Obviously, that had been enough

Love and Household Chores

In the old days on the farm there seemed to be a clear-cut separation between "his" duties and "hers." The wife was responsible for everything that went on inside the house, the man for everything outside. It is a wise and loving husband who has long since forgotten that outmoded idea. Now that the 140 acres outside have shrunk to a garage and a small yard, there is plenty of time to help the wife with the after-dinner dishes, take care of the children, and even change the baby's diapers. If his wife has to work outside the home, the husband's in-house chore responsibilities will increase. When the wife is expecting or after the baby arrives, it is again a tribute to his love when he willingly assumes some of those chores usually borne by the wife.

One word of caution is in order to the husband who wishes to show his love by helping around the house. Some wives, particularly in their youth, might interpret such will-ingness to help as an indication that the husband disap-proves of their homemaking. Avoid this implication at all cost! Additionally, keep in mind that she is the manager of the house, so don't attempt to overhaul her system of doing things as though you were in charge of the household chores. In responsibility this is her domain. If in love you wish to volunteer to supplement efforts around the house, then subordinate yourself to her plan and household procedures. You have not abdicated your responsibility as head of the home to help fulfill your wife's plans at home.

Management experts agree that one requirement of a good manager is that he first be a good follower. If your wife prefers to keep the everyday dishes high in the top cupboard where you have to stretch to get them, put them there. She doesn't tell you how to arrange your tools. You may in love try to suggest a more practical location, but be sure to take your tact pills before you do. Your thoughtful efforts to help out will usually be cheerfully accepted as long as you are willing to respect her household policies. Otherwise, your good deed can become a bone of contention.

Don't Be a Household Drone

Speaking of "bones of contention," I have observed during the past decade as I have traveled the country holding Family Life Seminars that a mounting source of irritation for wives, particularly those who have to work outside the home (which amounts to 71 percent today), is the husband who comes home from work and refuses to help out around the house. He may remind her of the old adage as he flicks on the TV: "Man works from sun to sun; a woman's work is never done." This attitude on the part of selfish husbands may well account for the growing spirit of anger I detect in wives.

This was reflected in a *USA Today* poll about three years back that showed the results of the following questions. "If you had it to do over again, would you marry the same person?" Fifty-one percent of the women said no, 72 percent of the men said yes. Then they asked the women the simple question, "Does your husband voluntarily help you around the house?" Comparing the answer to the first question with those who said their husbands did help around the house, the number of women who said they would marry the same man again jumped to 82 percent! That should say something to men about how important it is for them to help around the house voluntarily. Even more, it should tell men how important to their marriage are the voluntary acts of kindness that say to a wife "I love you!"

Make Time for Love

The pressurized age in which we live seriously infringes upon our free time. In spite of our push-button appliances and timesaving electronic gadgetry, we have no more spare time available to us than did our forefathers. Personally, I think we do more things than they did, but I'm not sure we get more accomplished. I read somewhere that in 1900 the average man traveled a little over 1000 miles annually; today almost all adult men average over 30,000 miles yearly. If that is true, they travel more every two years than Grandfather did in his lifetime. Often husbands get in such a hurry that they have no time for love. Many wives share a pet peeve: "My husband holds down two jobs [or one job and 13 hobbies] and has no time for me." I often find their claim justified. Without realizing it, his merry-go-round of activities has become more crowded and speeded up until he can't stop it. A wise husband schedules into his activity book periodic "mini honeymoons," occasional dinners out, or some "couple time." That is particularly needed after the children arrive. Tailor your outings to your budget, of course, but by all means have them. There is something exciting about a night in a motel without routine household distractions. It not only gives the couple a few hours to get reacquainted as persons, but it also puts the mystery and spark back into their love life. We recommend a special outing at least once a quarter—more often if you can afford it. To the wife it says, "I love you, and I enjoy spending time with you."

Don't Confuse Love and Sex

We have already seen that women have a greater need for love then men, as evidenced by the fact that God commanded husbands four times, "Love your wife!" Men, early in life, have a greater need for sex than love. If the man is not too careful, he can ruin his wife's response ability by making too many demands for sex without love. It is a wise man who learns that many times his wife just wants to be held, tenderly touched, and caressed. The problem is, when he does this, his motor starts up and pretty soon he is making it clear that he wants more than affections. Usually, if he will control that first urge and continue his tender touch, gradually her motor will begin to ignite—and they both win. Ten to 15 minutes of more touching often produces much more satisfying lovemaking.

Verbalize Your Love

Wherever I have the opportunity to share one important word of wisdom to husbands, it is: "Be careful to verbalize your love to your wife." A man often thinks that because he has little need for verbal reassurance of his wife's love, she is equally self-sufficient. Don't you believe it! Have you noticed how often a little girl will sit on her father's lap and ask, "Daddy, do you love me? Why don't you tell me?" In spite of their better-developed bodies and expensive hairdos, women still thrive on hearing you verbalize your love. The more romantically you do it, the better.

I'm not altogether sure why women have this need to hear their husbands say repeatedly, "I love you. I love you. I love you," but they do, so you might as well get used to it. Perhaps they are the ones who took the greatest risk in getting married, putting their absolute trust and confidence in their husbands at such an early age that they were probably the only ones who dreamed their husbands would ever amount to anything. They did it because they loved us and wanted us to love them in return. They need to be reassured regularly that we are keeping our part of the bargain.

As the parents of two married daughters, we can appreciate the beautiful story of the father who gave his daughter's husband-to-be a new pocket watch as a wedding gift. When the lad popped up the gold cover the first time, he saw these words written across the face: "Say something nice to Sally each day." That wise father knew that a daily verbalization of love will do much for a marriage.

In spite of his questionable character, I like Merlin's advice to King Arthur regarding his treatment of Lady Guinevere when she became his queen. He simply insisted, "Love her! Love her! Love her!" God said it even better: "Love [her] . . . as Christ also loved the church" (Ephesians 5:25).

The Husband as Family Provider

From the very beginning, man was given the responsi-bil-ity of being the family breadwinner. God said to Adam, "In the sweat of your face you shall eat bread" (Genesis 3:19). From that day on, the man has been accountable for both the financial provision and the psychological and physical pro-tection of his family. In the New Testament, men are taught: "But if anyone does not provide for his own, and especially for those of his household, he has denied the faith and is worse than an unbeliever" (1 Timothy 5:8).

Whenever the husband is not the primary breadwinner in his marriage, this deficiency becomes a serious threat to his role of leadership and personal self-esteem. There are temporary exceptions to this, of course, particularly when by mutual consent the wife works as the husband takes additional, specialized training. This is a wife's investment in their corporate good. But it should not be a permanent way of life. As a basic rule of thumb, the husband's income should provide food, shelter, and clothing. If the wife works, her job should be on a temporary basis for such things as a house down payment, furniture, tuition for the children, or those cash purchases which the husband's income cannot provide. If her salary becomes a regular part of their living or is used to increase their standard of living, it will usually be impossible for her ever to quit, even when the children arrive.

The man needs the sense of responsibility that comes with knowing his family is dependent on him for the necessities of life. One of the dreadful abuses of welfare is that it becomes a way of life when unskilled individuals find it more profitable not to work because their free government subsidy is greater than their earning capabilities. In the long run, such a subsidy is not "free" when given to the able-bodied, for it strips them of their manhood and self-respect. When that is gone, they have nothing.

The technology of our day has complicated man's role as provider. Unless he waits to marry until he develops a skill or profession, he and his wife must often delay their family far longer than God intended to allow him time to graduate. The ever-present specter of inflation further complicates that problem by putting house-buying beyond the reach of the average newlyweds. In spite of these and other serious problems today, a Christian man is likened in Scripture to a "heretic" if he doesn't trust God to enable him to find some means of providing for his wife and children, if physically able to do so.

Balancing the Spiritual and the Material

The Spirit-controlled family provider will not be a lazy man, nor will he be obsessed with materialism. Instead he will "seek first the kingdom of God and His righteousness, and all these things shall be added to [him]" (Matthew 6:33). Two things about that verse we must keep in mind. First, there is nothing wrong with a Christian man who is interested in business success. But when his interest in business overshadows his love for spiritual things, both he and the family are in trouble. Second, God will not supply him with everything on a silver platter. The divine command to Adam is still basic: Man is to earn his bread by the sweat of his face. Through the years I have noticed that every time I asked God to supply a special need in our family's life, He did so by giving me some extra work that brought in additional income. Rarely did His answer come like "manna from heaven." Men tend toward extremes, and Satan will try to destroy them first by the extreme of laziness. I have found some men who were content to float through life simply because they were lazy. For over a year I tried to help a 40-year-old father of four children learn a profession. Finally, at the urging of some of my associates, we let him go. He frequently came in late, puttered unproductively, and was the first to leave in the evening. It simply cost us too much money to keep him. The difficult life to which he is needlessly subjecting his family is an example of selfish laziness, which is reprehensible for a Christian.

The second extreme is much more common: the Christian man who hides behind his work to avoid cultivating his spiritual life or that of his family. Workaholics are not Spirit-controlled; they are self-driven. One of the consistent traits of a Spirit-controlled husband and father is that, although he works hard and may occasionally endure heavy work-pressure periods, his work does not take priority over his family.

In this connection I have watched a few Christian men make the mistake of working every Sunday. One such manager of a supermarket made double-time pay for Sunday work and concluded that his family needed the money. He rarely came to church, though many times he assured me that he "loved the Lord." Naturally, he experienced an underdeveloped spiritual life, and his home showed it. His three girls grew up with little interest in the things of the Lord, rarely attended church, and married unsaved men. I last saw him for counseling because his wife was running around with another man. I consider that an expensive price to pay for double-time wages.

I see nothing wrong with a Christian businessman working occasionally on Sunday. Even the Old Testament taught that when the ox fell into the ditch on the Sabbath, the farmer was to get him out, no matter how messy and muddy the task. But any Christian man who must work every Sunday, forcing him to absent himself consistently from the Lord's house, has the wrong job. I have seen men trust God for real miracles in this connection and find that He always supplies their needs. Happy is the man who understands that his vocation is a trust from God. His talents, energy, and creativity are gifts from God and should be used for His glory. No man has ever been shortchanged if he puts the Lord first vocationally.

The cover of the March 13, 1995 edition of *U.S. News* featured the picture of the wealthy Christian businessman Norman Miller with a Bible in his hand. The article told the success stories of several "born-again businessmen" who used their businesses to promote their faith. I happen to personally know three of the men mentioned. They are all dedicated Christians, but I can also testify that all three have worked hard for what God has blessed them with. It is a matter of balance. God told Adam he was to "earn his bread by the sweat of his face." God promised to "supply all your need." He means He will give you an opportunity to trust Him to earn your own bread by hard work. It's part of being a human being.

Chapter 8

The Husband as Teacher, Priest, and Protector

*T*he first commandment God gave to Adam and Eve was, "Be fruitful and multiply; fill the earth" (Genesis 1:28). Since that time, fatherhood has played a major role in the life of husbands and has been a rich source of blessing to men who have taken this additional role seriously. In recent years, modern science has put into the hands of young couples birth-control techniques which enable them to limit the size of their family and, in a surprising number of cases, avoid having children altogether. Humanistically oriented educators' and population experts' warnings that we must reduce the size of our families have been so well received in America that the number of children per family dropped to 1.6 in 1994. This attitude is gaining popularity even among Christian families, in spite of the priority the Bible and Christianity have always placed on the family. The words of the psalmist need to be pondered by every prospective parent: "Children are a heritage from the Lord: the fruit of the womb is His reward. . . . Happy is the man who has his quiver full of them" (Psalm 127:3,5). An old Hebrew tradition tells us that a quiver which soldiers carried to war was large enough to contain five arrows. Could this suggest that, since children are such a blessing, a man would be fully happy with five of them?

Bev and I are somewhat biased on this subject because God gave us four children to raise, and one was lost prior to birth. We certainly can testify that children raised in the Lord are a blessing. God has showered us with far more blessings in our lives than we ever dreamed possible, but we have none that even come close to the treasures bearing our children's names (unless it is our nine grandchildren). We are always saddened when we meet young couples who cheat themselves out of this greatest of all blessings in life. Almost anyone can propagate children, but raising them is a different matter. Fatherhood takes hard work, sacrifice, and time, but it is its own reward.

The Nature of Fatherhood

The Spirit-controlled father does not lack specific instructions from the Word of God as to the true nature of his duties. Ephesians 6:4 states, "And you, fathers, do not provoke your children to wrath, but bring them up in the training and admonition of the Lord." There are three classic commands in this verse which we will consider individually.

1. *Fathers are to love their children.* "Do not provoke your children to wrath." Every child needs love and intuitively seeks it from his parents. If his love is rejected or if Mom and Dad do not exhibit affection, he is filled with wrath. Anyone who studies the juvenile scene today, noting the hostility that emanates from teenagers and the high rate of rejection or negligence among their parents, must recognize that we are raising a generation of love-starved children.

When I did the research for *The Unhappy Gays: What Everyone Should Know About Homosexuality*, I was amazed to find that all homosexuals are filled with hostility. I have already acknowledged my own former problems with anger and have majored in counseling hostile married couples and individuals, so I think I know a little about choleric wrath. But I have never seen anything like the homosexual brand of hostility. And what is the number-one cause? A rejecting father. One former homosexual, now a minister who is helping men come out of that unhappy lifestyle, said, "I have counseled over 300 homosexuals and have yet to find one who experienced a good relationship with his father."

A juvenile-court judge, after presiding over thousands of juvenile cases, observed, "I have yet to see a boy come before my court who had a father who took him fishing or went to ball games or spent time with him." It has been my observation that the father who demonstrates his love for his children by making time for teaching them, no matter how busy his schedule, enjoys his children when they are adults. That doesn't mean they will never stir up a fuss and manifest their all-too-human nature. However, the wise man of Proverbs assures us that although "foolishness is bound up in the heart of a child," we can be certain that "the rod of correction will drive it far from him" (Proverbs 22:15). Even the children of a loving, Spirit-controlled father may store a degree of foolishness in their hearts, which sooner or later will reveal itself in wrath. But the anger in their spirits will be much less severe and more short-lived than that of the child whose father has provoked him to wrath by neglecting to supply his need for love.

One of my dearest friends is a motorcycle nut. He has won almost every trophy a champion cycle racer can win. His garage contains more motorcycles than his house has people (and he is raising a large family). His oldest son was early introduced to a "dirt bike" (they never ride on the street for fear some fool driver will kill them), and together they have spent thousands of hours riding, repairing their machines, and planning the next Baja trip. But then the boy started running around with the wrong crowd and succeeded in getting himself kicked out of our Christian high school. Some tense months followed for two prayerfully concerned parents. The inevitable dope scene which forms a part of the public high schools in our community was drawing the lad into its orbit when suddenly, like the prodigal son, he came to himself. The father and the boy continued to ride and work on their bikes, and Dad wisely avoided nagging his son about his activities. Eventually, the teenager realized that Dad was the best friend he had on this earth. He rededicated his life to Christ, gave up his old friends, and eventually married a lovely Christian girl. Father-love won again!

2. *Fathers are to teach their children.* If there is a consistent neglect among conscientious fathers today, it is in facing their responsibility as teachers of their children. Because Mother is the primary teacher during the first few years of a youngster's life, many men never assume their proper teaching role when the children get older. The Scripture clearly states that fathers are to bring up their children in the nurture of the Lord—that is, train them by example and precept in the ways of God.

Children do not tell the truth by nature, nor do they automatically share or act responsibly. These are principles that must be instilled by example and precept. In addition, children must be taught skills commensurate with their age and sex. Unfortunately, the electronic advances of our age often create tools that are far too sophisticated for young boys in the learning stage. In the old days, life was simple. A father only had a few tools, all of which his son could be taught to use at an early age. But today's power equipment presents special problems. Yet children must learn, and Father is their best instructor. If he spends time teaching skills, sports, and social customs, his children will readily listen while he imparts to them the principles of character and the statutes of God.

3. *Fathers are to discipline their children.* The hardest job in the whole business of fatherhood is discipline. Without it, however, there is no such thing as successful parenthood. We hear a great deal about child abuse today, as both the opinion molders of the media and federal bureaucrats have discovered yet another crisis that can be manipulated to trick the American people into succumbing to additional legislative interference in their personal lives. This one is more valid than the energy crisis, however, for as any hospital emergency-ward doctor will acknowledge, child abuse is on the increase. What would make an adult lash out at and strike a helpless infant or child? The answer: the frustration of rage in an undisciplined person who has lost control. Usually the product of a rejecting or permissive home, the parent cannot endure the pressure which endless crying or childish annoyance brings. Few child-beaters are really murderers at heart, but all are selfish, angry, undisciplined people who themselves were abused in childhood. They are almost as pathetic as the children they beat.

However, as tragic as that kind of child abuse may be, another variety is far more common and less publicized. Consider carefully the children whose lives are destroyed through lack of parental discipline. Their number is legion! Most penitentiaries, juvenile halls, houses of correction, and cemeteries are full of them. Many others are borderline casualties who marry and divorce several times, father and abandon children, and are unable to keep a job. Such human tragedies could easily have been avoided had their fathers heeded the biblical injunction that a father who truly loves his son will discipline him.

Self-discipline, self-denial, and self-control are absolute essentials in maturing to adulthood. A father cannot possibly prepare his children educationally or vocationally for all the complex changes that await them in the twenty-first century. For instance, many present-day vocations will be automated out of existence. One thing a father can do for his children however, is provide exactly what they need to prepare for whatever uncertainties lurk ahead. He can teach them discipline. The foundation for self-discipline is *parental* discipline. The child who is lovingly disciplined in the home will much more readily make the transition to self-discipline when he is older. The child raised without practical discipline is not only "provoked to wrath," but his lack of self-control also contributes to his self-destruction or, at best, self-limitation.

When I was active in Christian Heritage College, we often saw the difference that self-discipline makes. The most tragic waste of human talent and opportunity involves young people who lack sufficient self-discipline to be finishers. We taught our students that they shouldn't take all the easy courses, but rather try to select at least one difficult subject a year, for a passing grade in that class would build character, which is far more beneficial than knowledge. To be sure, knowledge is important, but character is far more so, because it determines what you do with what you know. No matter how much you know, nothing is more important than what you are. There is no substitute for Christian character. But waiting until you can send your child away to a Christian college, with the hope that the school will accomplish what you failed to achieve, is abdicating your role as a father.

Several years ago the Houston, Texas, police department published a list of "Twelve Rules for Raising Delinquent Children." These rules verify that the police, who have to work with the products of permissiveness, were never deceived by the ivory-tower theorists and the trusting parents who believed the notion that children are born good and need to grow up expressing their goodness.

Twelve Rules for Raising Delinquent Children

1. Begin with infancy to give the child everything he wants. In this way he will grow up believing the world owes him a living.

2. When he picks up bad words, laugh at him. This will make him think he's cute. It will also encourage him to pick up "cuter" phrases that will blow off the top of your head later.

3. Never give him any spiritual training. Wait till he is 21 and then let him "decide for himself."

4. Avoid use of the word "wrong." It may develop a guilt complex. This will condition him to believe later, when he is arrested for stealing a car, that society is against him and he is being persecuted.

5. Pick up everything he leaves lying around: books, shoes, and clothing. Do everything for him so he will be experienced in throwing all responsibility onto others.

6. Let him read any printed matter he can get his hands on. Be careful that the silverware and drinking glasses are sterilized, but let his mind feast on garbage.

7. Quarrel frequently in the presence of your children. In this way they will not look shocked when the home is broken up later.

8. Give a child all the spending money he wants. Never let him earn his own. Why should he have things as tough as you had them?

9. Satisfy his every craving for food, drink, and comfort. See that every sensual desire is gratified. Denial may lead to harmful frustration.

10. Take his part against neighbors, teachers, and policemen. They are all prejudiced against your child.

11. When he gets into real trouble, apologize for yourself by saying, "I never could do anything with him."

12. Prepare for a life of grief. You will be apt to have it.

The techniques of child-raising were covered quite thoroughly by Bev in *How to Develop Your Child's Temperament,* where she applies the biblical principles of discipline not only to the four temperaments but also to the various ages of children and teens, so we shall not repeat them here. But it is important, Dad, to point out two final principles about fathering. First, it is your responsibility from God to see that your children are well-disciplined. Your wife may do it when they are small or when you're away, but you should see to it that they are disciplined in love. Second, you must be an example of what you teach. Nothing turns young people off faster than hypocrisy, and teaching one thing while doing another qualifies as hypocrisy.

While I was still active as senior pastor of a great church, Bev and I were invited to attend a social activity in the home of one of my associate pastors. I happened to be within easy earshot when his teenage son answered the phone. He told the party on the other end that his father was busy and couldn't come to the phone, but the caller persisted. To the young man's credit, he was equally persistent and politely offered to take the number and have his father call later. As he hung up the phone, his friend said, "Why didn't you just tell them he wasn't home and avoid all that hassle?" The teen replied, "My father wouldn't like that; it isn't true." That boy will never have to take a course in basic honesty! Interestingly enough, that young man has just gone through one of the most difficult trials a man can face: the unexpected death of his wife, leaving him with a five-month-old son. He is facing that trial with genuine character, hammered out on the anvil of home integrity.

What Will Your Children Say?

Sixteen Christians attending a home Bible study were asked the question, "What was your father like?" One said, "He was a loving, tender guy." Another commented that her dad was a dedicated Christian who loved her very much. Some reported they "never really knew" their dad, and so on around the group. Not one person mentioned the father's profession, possessions, or position in life. If the Lord tarries and you depart this life before your family, what will they say about you? You aren't impressing them with what you do for a living, but by what you are. Who are you?

The Husband as Family Priest

The most neglected role of the husband is one that predominated in ancient days—that of family priest. In Ephesians 5 we are told that the husband is to the wife what Christ is to the church. If Christ is our high priest, then, husband, you are the priest of your home. All spiritual instruction is your responsibility.

You are probably aware that in many homes the mother takes care of the religious training of the children, which she can pursue during their early years. If the father has no interest in spiritual things, when the children reach their teens, the spiritual mortality rate is extremely high.

When your wife conceived the children who bear your name, more was brought into this world than mind, emotions, and body. People are uniquely different from animals, for they possess a distinct spiritual side to their nature which needs cultivation by training and exercise. Far too many Christian fathers think they have fulfilled their responsibility by providing food, shelter, love, and discipline for their children. But this would neglect the spiritual potential of both the wife and children. It is your responsibility to lead them in the paths of the Lord. Consider the following ways a father fulfills his family priesthood:

1. *He will be a Spirit-controlled man.* This, of course, is the foundation of the Christian father's priesthood, as it is in every other role.

2. *He will be regular in his daily Bible reading.* We have found that children who see their father

feed daily on the Word of God and incorporate its teachings into his life are easily taught this daily practice in their youth. More is "caught" in this area than "taught."

3. *He will lead in family devotions.* It seems incredible to me that any Spirit-controlled family would not spend some time each day in Bible reading and prayer.

We found it best to tailor the devotional time to the age of the children. When they were small, we read a short passage of Scripture, taught one of them to pray, and then closed the session with prayer. As they grew older, we enlarged the Scripture reading and let them take part. In their junior and teen years, we would often discuss the scriptural passage and have at least three participate in prayer. Today you may wish to make use of the excellent devotional helps and materials available in Christian bookstores. They also carry exciting children's stories that maintain the interest of toddlers. We found these to be excellent for story time during the evening or just before bed.

A pastor friend in the Midwest has a devotional system that may be even better than the one we used. Every night the family has devotions together just before the children go to bed. Dad leads when home; if he's away, his wife leads in Bible reading and prayer. If both parents are away, their oldest son leads. When he is gone, the next oldest is in charge. All baby-sitters are instructed in the procedure, so that every night ends in family prayer. If our children were still home, we would try this procedure. The family prayer and Bible-reading time, often called "the family altar" or "family devotions," can best be led by Dad. He has the more commanding voice, and it is good for the children to know that Dad is 100 percent behind a program of building spirituality into the lives of his children.

I had the joy of seeing what I call a "Texas wastrel" (a man who had wasted his life on the sins of the flesh) come to

Christ. Sometime after his conversion, we were discussing why he came to a minister while half-drunk and obviously on the bottom rung of life. "It was the old family Bible my father read from each night. I turned my back on my father's faith, but I always knew it was available if I ever got desperate."

That kind of confidence has stood many a child in good stead when tempted by sin, philosophy, and materialism. It is the father-priest of the home who should lead in such devotional times. Admittedly, some temperaments find it harder to conduct such sessions than others. Your family, however, doesn't need a polished speaker at that moment, but priestly leadership in Bible reading and prayer by the most important person in their lives. It isn't how you do it that is important; it's who you are.

Practical Suggestions for the Devotional Hour

To make those devotional times as effective as possible, we offer the following suggestions:

1. *Plan a time that best fits the schedule of your family.* This may change as your children grow or when Dad has to work a different shift. But there should be one special time when the family can include a 10- to 30-minute family session in their program. We found that for us, right after the evening meal was usually the best time. Everyone was relaxed and in a good mood to talk to God.

2. *Be consistent but not legalistic.* Occasionally, an important Little League game will be missed unless you skip devotions, but as a rule, at least five nights a week should find the family sharing their devotional time together.

3. *It takes cooperation from both Mother and Dad for this program to be consistent.* Mother must start the meal on time so it doesn't run into other scheduled activities. (Many a Christian

wife grumbles at her husband's inconsistency, without realizing that the lateness of the evening meal often contributes to the devotional neglect.) Dad should gather the Bible and/or devotional materials and mentally prepare for devotions, perhaps reading over the Bible portion before dinner.

4. *Encourage the children to take part.* Father doesn't have to read the Scripture and direct the session every time, but the children should understand what has been read.

5. *Use this time to teach the family to pray.* Like many families, we installed a cork bulletin board on our kitchen wall and posted a world map pinpointing the missionaries our church supports. To this we added others who had visited our home and our special requests for prayer. It was always a blessing to the children to formally thank God for His answer when it came, at which time we removed the request from the board.

Praying comes easily for children when, as far back as they can remember, grace was said at each meal and talking to Jesus was as natural as talking to anyone else. Our own children still have no difficulty expecting God's answers to prayer, for they traced His faithfulness to our family many times. One occasion comes to mind. I have always believed in sharing our needs with the family and, whenever possible, visualizing our request to make it more specific. Our car was about to gasp its last breath, so we discussed buying a new one. We all decided that our family of six needed a nine-passenger station wagon. We even picked out a three-seat Plymouth which featured a special door and electronic window. Naturally, it had to feature an automatic transmission and all the "extras." By the time we added the requirements together, the car was far too expensive for our meager budget, so we began to ask God for a good used one. When I found a beautiful picture in a magazine of just what we wanted, we cut it out and pinned it on our prayer board. Each night the children remembered to pray for the car. Frankly, at times their faith was stronger than mine, because that model of car was less than a year old, and used ones were as scarce as hens' teeth.

One evening the phone rang. A Navy chief who attended another church in our city heard we were looking for a good used car and called to ask us if we would like to buy his. He was being sent overseas and had a "seven-month-old Plymouth station wagon." I was almost too nervous to ask if it was a nine-passenger model with three seats, but of course it was. We bought the car by taking over his payments—the best car buy we ever made. That car transported our family for over five years and remains the one car that stands out in the children's minds to this day. Three of our children are married, with children of their own, and all have cars they prayed into their families. We taught our children to pray about everything from clothes to houses to parking spaces. We also taught them Scripture verses like: "Until now you have asked nothing in My name. Ask, and you will receive, that your joy may be full" (John 16:24).

The father-priest who faithfully fulfills his spiritual responsibilities to his family lives to enjoy his children later in life. You probably know many fathers who wish they could experience those young, pliable years all over again. But once passed, they are gone forever. The father-priest who does his work faithfully fashions a spiritual belt of protection that will protect his children all through life. The priestly ministry of the father is a reinforcement every family needs to assure the successful raising of their children.

The Husband as Family Protector

As far back as anthropologists go in their research, man has always been the protector of his family. When we were in Africa last year, we saw a typical native scene—a small village of five huts, all surrounded by a handmade wall with only one gate. As we stepped inside, there sat the father, bow across his lap, obviously protecting the homes of his five wives and 29 children.

The need for physical protection varies with the community and the man's means and opportunity. It is so basically understood in our society that we need only mention some of the less obvious but equally important areas in which a husband is the family protector.

1. *He will protect his wife psychologically.* We have already seen that self-acceptance and self-respect are essential to every human being. What you think of yourself influences everything you do. In fact, what you think of yourself is far more important than what you suppose other people think of you. To a wife, her husband's opinion of her is of vital importance. For if he approves of her, it matters little who does not; but if he does not esteem her, it doesn't matter who else does.

Every wise husband will go out of his way, as we saw in our study of love, to encourage his wife with his approval. The Bible says a husband should "honor . . . the wife as . . . the weaker vessel" (1 Peter 3:7). You have, no doubt, seen a man publicly humiliate his wife in front of mutual friends by sarcastically announcing her weaknesses or by subjecting her to other forms of ill-advised ridicule. Sanguine men do it because they are tactless and egocentric; consequently, they will say anything to get a laugh. Melancholies criticize everything and everyone (unless they're filled with the Spirit), so their wives are no exception. No one can be more sarcastic than a choleric. He often has the mistaken idea that hanging his wife's undesirable traits out to dry before his friends may induce her to "shape up." Of all the temperaments, phlegmatics are least likely to criticize their wives in public, but they also are seldom heard to say something complimentary.

A MelChlor husband came in for counseling several times. He was both critical and sarcastic (a devastating formula for ruining a wife), but he knew he should change.

According to his official report, his SanPhleg little wife "did everything wrong." As a highly successful businessman who ran a very efficient office (with the aid of a secretary who could put up with him in short doses), he could not understand why his wife failed to do the same at home. He confessed, however, that his way of dealing with the situation was making matters worse. You guessed it: His management technique required him to criticize her from the moment he came in from work until they went to bed. "You don't keep the house straight." "The kitchen is disorganized." "The family records are a disaster." "You ruin the gas dryer by never cleaning the lint remover." "You can't even fold my socks right." To no one's surprise, their love life had dipped to zero. I asked him if he had ever tried *praise*. "Of course not," came the reply. "I never have anything to praise her for!" "Has your wife ever been unfaithful?" I asked. "No," he answered.

Further questioning supplied the following information: She had borne him three children, served fairly good meals, was a dedicated Christian, loved and was good to his mother, dressed his kids well, and helped them with their homework. "But she is such a messy housekeeper!" he interjected. His tunnel vision could only focus on this glaring weakness, making him impervious to the fact that his criticism, nagging, and harping were only making things worse. Fortunately, in his desperate straits he was willing to try anything, even praise.

We worked out a plan that called for 30 days of praise. It took all the self-control he could muster, but he fulfilled his assignment and then furnished this report: "The first four days she didn't know what to expect, but gradually she relaxed. On the fifth day she met me at the door with a kiss, which she hadn't done in years. She started cooking my favorite foods again and actually put my laundry in the drawer before I got home. Last week some gal loaned her a book called *The Total Woman*, and one night, when the kids were at my mother's, you wouldn't believe how she met me at the door!" He never mentioned whether her house-keeping was improving (it probably was), but somehow I don't think it mattered anymore.

One of the secondary meanings for the biblical word *submission* involves being "responsive" or "a responder." A woman is a responder to her husband's treatment. I have never seen a woman fail to respond affirmatively to love, kindness, and praise.

2. *He will protect his children psychologically.* No man looms more important in the heart of children than their father. Consequently, what he thinks of them is of paramount significance in their formative years. It is essential that fathers learn to gear down to the level of the children's characters and encourage or praise them in all that they do. Like a wife, children respond positively to praise but never to criticism.

Every young man I have met with a good self-image has testified to a loving father who spent time with him and was more approving and encouraging than he was critical. Most young men get their attitude toward themselves from their father.

3. *He will protect his family from philosophical error.* The world in which we live is engaged in a battle for control of the human mind, and every Christian father ought to be aware of this. God is using the Bible, the church, and the home to build into the minds of children those principles they need to enable them to live properly in this life and eternity. Satan, on the other hand, uses everything at his disposal to corrupt the minds of our children and to inflame their youthful passions in order to wrest them from the plan and purpose of God. He has seized our once-great school system and now uses it to propagate atheism, evolution, amorality, free love, debilitating drugs, and other unbelievably evil philosophies. He also has appropriated

TV, movies, books, magazines, and other media that reach into the mind. The Spirit-filled father will recognize these prime sources of evil and keep them out of his house. Since children will not instinctively exercise good judgment and seem to be mesmerized by that which is harmful, God gave them parents to govern their decisions.

A few years ago, naive parents used to argue with me when I suggested that they censor the TV in their home. The "tube" has become so corrupt and degenerate that parents no longer deny its effect. Hollywood's exaltation of immorality, lesbianism, and homosexuality has revealed it for the entertainment corrupter it has always been. "Man's ways are not God's ways," and Christian parents ought to face it. We cannot trust Satan to entertain or educate our families.

A pastor friend from Oklahoma once invited the superintendent of our Christian school system in San Diego and me to speak in his church on a Wednesday evening in an attempt to encourage his congregation to begin a Christian school in the community. He asked me privately if it was appropriate for him to be motivated because of his concern for the influence of secular education upon his own children. I laughed and then explained, "That is exactly why we started Christian High School of San Diego many years ago. I was concerned about the evil philosophy my children were exposed to at school, day after day." That pastor didn't realize it, but he was revealing that he had his priorities straight; he is a father first and a pastor second.

Every father ought to be concerned about the kind of education his children are receiving. If it exercises an unwholesome influence on them (and it probably does, now that the federal government controls our local schools through federal funding), he ought to do everything within his power to provide his children with a Christian education. I am convinced that every Bible-believing church in America ought to consider using its facilities for a weekday

Christian school. According to the latest local education tests, we do a far better job of education than the public school, and our children are safer from physical, moral, and philosophical harm. In addition, we can teach them the Bible. Churches without adequate facilities to provide more than one or two classrooms ought to cooperate with other churches of like mind.

What about the expense of private education? With most parents this is a vital factor. But God has promised He will provide all our needs, and if you recognize this as a need and make it an earnest matter of prayer, God will supply the means. Many of the parents who sent their children to Christian schools thought they could never afford it, but God has provided miracle after miracle. Never limit God through unbelief by deciding in advance what He cannot do. (That's why the children of Israel spent 40 years in the desert unnecessarily.)

For those who do not have access to a Christian school in their community or definitely cannot afford it unless Mother works outside the home, we suggest you consider home schooling. Yes, teach them yourself in the home. We know—you probably feel unqualified. Most parents do. The truth is, between 700,000 and one million children are being home schooled today, and academic tests prove that most are doing it very well. We have an overexaggerated assumption that the public schools are doing a good job with all their billions of dollars. However, academic tests don't reveal that! And the violence, immorality, and antireligious and sometimes antiparent teaching that goes on makes it very risky. In most cases, well-disciplined home schooling by parents is better academically, spiritually, and morally than even the best public schools. For information on home schooling contact:

Christian Home Educators Association
P.O. Box 2009
Norwalk, CA 90651
(800) 564-CHEA
(ask for the manual "An Introduction to
Home Education")

The National Center for Home Education
P.O. Box 125
Paeonian Springs, VA 22129

The Home School Legal Defense
P.O. Box 159
Paeonian Springs, VA 22129

4. *He will protect his wife and children from disrespect.* The rebellion that lurks in the heart of all children will ultimately surface in the home. That rebellion usually takes its first form in disrespect toward their mother. When children are small, minor insubordination will be treated as disobedience by Mom, but if not squelched early, it becomes a habit that only the father can cure. If he does not, that disrespect will eventually be turned on him, then directed outside the home, and will finally pit the child against society and the police. Rarely do police officers have to arrest respectful children.

My father had only an eighth-grade education and died of a heart attack at 34 years of age, so I don't remember a great deal about him. But I do recall how he taught me to always respect my mother. I came home from school one day when I was in the fourth grade and said something sassy and disrespectful to my mother. I did not realize my father was already home! Suddenly, I heard my name called from the other room where he was reading. You know the sound—icicles fell from each letter of my name as he said it. Immediately, I went into the other room and said, "Yes, sir!"

Then he said, "Young man, I want you to go back in the kitchen and apologize to your mother. And if I ever hear you speak to her again that way, there will be a hole in the wall just your size!" I got the message! My mother lived to be 81 and never heard me speak to her that way again.

Needless to say, my mother loved my father while she had him. And both of us treasured the rest of our lives the memory of a man who demanded respect for the woman who bore his children. I have a hunch that there would be fewer teenage rebels today if their fathers had demanded respect for the parents before the children were 12. The child with a sassy mouth is reflecting the fact that he has a sassy heart. For the Bible says, "Out of the abundance of the heart the mouth speaks" (Matthew 12:34).

No one but the father can guarantee that the children of the home will respect their mother, provided he speaks respectfully of her himself. I have raised my children that way. To this day, my sons, who are very fond of their mother and always relaxed around her, may tease her but they are never disrespectful.

The husband who loves the Lord and his wife will guarantee her that respect. The Lord requires it when he says, "Likewise you husbands, dwell with them with understanding, giving honor to the wife, as to the weaker vessel . . . that your prayers may not be hindered" (1 Peter 3:7).

The Art of
Family Communication

*C*ommunication is a basic part of all human life. It is one of the significant differences separating people from animals. Man has an innate desire for communication with both God and his fellowman. Many individuals substitute communicating with their fellow humans for communication with God. Ultimately, this is self-destructive because it tends to be communication for selfish purposes. Individuals who genuinely enjoy communication with God through the power of His indwelling Spirit will be more relaxed about themselves and others; consequently, they find it easier to communicate with those around them.

The experts in communication point out that this art con-tains three basic elements: 1) talking, 2) listening, and 3) understanding. We could add two more important ingredients: body language and empathy. Everyone knows how to define *talking*, but talking does not guarantee communication. As Dr. Howard Hendricks has often said at our seminars, "Talking is easy; anyone can do it. But communication is hard work." And we could add that communication requires two people, both concentrating on the same thing: that which is being said.

Because talking is so much easier than listening, the hardest problem in the whole process is listening. If the listener isn't interested in the subject and has no motivation to pay attention, communication is almost impossible. As a public speaker, I have long assumed that communication is the responsibility of the speaker. But after teaching on both the high school and college level for years, I finally came to realize that the best visualized presentation (with printouts included) will not be understood without the cooperation of the listener.

If that is true generally, it is even more so in a family situation. Communication always requires at least two people. One of the most advertised problems in marriage is that of communication breakdown. If active marriage counselors were polled, the top two problems would be family finances and communication. Though counselors may differ on which is number one, most would rate one of these two areas first and the other second. One expert suggests that 50 percent of all marriages have a serious communication problem. And Christians are not exempt.

Recently, Bev and I counseled an active church couple with several children. One of their illustrations was that the wife had driven off on Sunday evening without asking if he wanted to attend the choir's performance of the cantata in which she was singing. He was upset because she hadn't asked his desire but assumed he didn't wish to attend. He angrily said, "I always attend Sunday-night services!" Communication was so painful for this couple that both had avoided sharing their true feelings.

Gradual Communication Difficulties

It has long been a phenomenon in marriage counseling that couples who never have a difficult time communicating before marriage can develop such communication difficulties afterward. Even couples who maintain, "We still love each other deeply!" can find communication difficult. Before marriage they could talk endlessly about everything (particularly on the phone while the girl's father was trying to call home), but gradually after marriage it becomes more difficult until it develops into a serious problem. How did it happen? Very gradually. The following are some of the things that slowly stifle conversation between two love-birds after the honeymoon.

1. *Differing perspectives.* Prior to marriage, the couple shared a common dream: their ultimate marriage and home. After marriage, the young man is faced with new responsibilities and restrictions that cause him to concentrate on supporting his wife, and sometimes he even questions whether or not it's worth it in the light of these restrictions. At 20 or so years of age, he had finally earned the right to come and go in his home or apartment without having to give an account of his time or activities. Suddenly, he's confronted with a wife who wants to know, "When will you be home? . . . Where will you be? . . . *Who* are you going out with?" Very gradually, the novelty of married life is replaced by a feeling of irritation at this new requirement of accountability. Vocationally, the husband begins to shift into a higher gear than during the courtship days, when he had somewhat sidestepped his vocational interests (not the work or, in the case of the student, his studies. But they were not number one in his mind—getting married was). Now he returns to a basic need: vocational aptitude and financial solvency. Prior to marriage, their number-one interest was shared equally. Now he goes off alone into a different world. She may ask, "How did it go at school [or work] today?" and he may give a five- or ten-minute answer. But he spent eight to ten hours of his life at it, apart from her. The wife, if she does not work outside the home, becomes domesticated in her thinking, concentrating on meals, clothes, house, and so on. If she divides herself between vocational and domesticated

thoughts, the young bride also may be somewhat disillusioned at the realities of marriage. Rushing home from work to plan meals, instead of eating Mother's cooking, takes getting used to. It is not uncommon for two lovers to sit at home in silence within weeks after the wedding, both silently questioning the rightness of their decision, but unwilling to discuss their true feelings. This period is usually temporary and is the initial phase of adjustment. It is important that the couple talk honestly and freely during these days, but it's not easy.

2. *Different primary interests and involvements.* It is natural for a young married woman to begin thinking of motherhood. As she does, and particularly after becoming pregnant, her number-one interest is the baby (and the home). His number-one concern is increasingly vocational, especially if they are taking on the additional responsibilities of parenthood. As such, the books and magazines he reads are vocational; hers are family-centered. Her thoughts become immediate; his increasingly long-range. While she is thinking of "bassinets and buntings," he is thinking of "a place in the suburbs." They begin to put priorities on different things. She may feel that his reluctance to spend money for the nursery shows a disinterest in the baby. If she verbalizes such an idea, he may become offended. He is apt to feel that her desire to buy furniture for the baby now is unreasonable in the light of saving for a down payment on their new home. Different marital priorities produce conflicts of interest.

One of the reasons we favor the Lamaze birth program, becoming so popular today, is that it forces the couple to prepare *together* for the baby's arrival. It affords them a vital opportunity to share something intimately at a time when they need something to share. Unfortunately, hospitals indicate that many husbands are difficult to persuade to take the training. This mutual interest, though valuable, is often short-lived. They need other areas of interest to share.

A deep marital companionship and friendship must be built on mutual interests. Whenever I see a husband and wife who do not share common goals and interests, I look for trouble. If all they share is the same name, house, bed, and children, they will gradually grow apart. They must develop common interests.

That is where the church and mutual spiritual interests greatly aid the Spirit-controlled couple. Regular study of the Word, Christian friends, and other Christ-related activities are a real asset. A woman, particularly in the early days of marriage, would be wise to learn as much as possible about her husband's work, his favorite sports, and the daily news, if those are his chief areas of interest. It is a wise husband who also cultivates his wife's interests and keeps up with her reading levels. One of the reasons seminaries have special classes for "seminary wives" is that so many couples have such a diversity of interests during the husband's three years in school because the wife is not studying the Bible along with her husband.

Another factor in this connection is friends. Unless they are strong Christians, couples are apt to make new friendships with others who are not interested in spiritual things. The young wife, confined to the home and usually without transportation, has to make friends in her apartment or neighborhood. The husband makes new friends in his changing classes at school or at work. Consequently, it is not uncommon for the former "inseparables" to desire different nights out with their work or neighborhood associates. This can be dangerous.

3. *Opposite temperaments affect communication.* Temperament influences everything in a person's life, particularly conversation. What appears clever and cute before marriage may be irritating afterward. Sanguines are supertalkers. Their motto is: "When in doubt, talk," or as a sanguine friend of mine said, "Sanguines enter a room mouth first!" That is

only true when they have an audience for which to perform. Prior to marriage, they go into their act for their "intended." After they have said everything they know three times, they begin to be silent until a visitor arrives. That makes the spouse resentful that the sanguine "talks more when a stranger is here than when we are alone."

Cholerics talk continuously about business, are opinionated, and often thrive on argumentation. It is difficult to talk to a choleric. If you disagree, he baits you into verbal argument. If you concur, there isn't much to say which he hasn't already stated. Warning: Disagree with a choleric at your own risk! No one can be more sarcastic and caustic.

Melancholies are verbal perfectionists with a built-in obsession to be precise and to correct everyone else's way of doing things. They take disagreement extremely personally and often read into what you say exactly what you *meant* but didn't want to say (and sometimes what you don't mean).

Phlegmatics are not supertalkers. They let others speak, evaluate the whole scene, and rarely disagree for fear of criticism or conflict. Fortunately, they are extremely diplomatic. Were it not for that, their partners might have them in verbal confrontations all the time.

These temperament differences only expose the vast thinking differences which most couples possess. There is a need to learn to see life through the partner's eyes.

4. *One- or two-celled thinking patterns affect communication.* Another subtle difference between couples in marriage is the ability to think of more than one thing at a time. Bev has the ability to carry on eight things at once. Not me! I can think of only one subject at a time. I came home one night to find her caring for our grandchildren who had Tupperware all over the floor. She had a cake in the oven, was cooking something on the stove, and while setting the table had the telephone nestled against her ear listening to

an endless conversation. As I went by she whispered, "Hi!" and puckered up for a kiss. I can't do that. When you talk to me on the phone, you either get my undivided attention or nothing.

This characteristic is probably more a result of differences in temperament than due to sexual identity. Usually men are considered more single-celled in their thinking, but I'm not sure that is true. We have an attorney friend who reads legal briefs while watching TV. Bev can do that, but neither his wife nor I can. Bev used to get annoyed at me because I wouldn't talk to her during a TV program. I can't do it. In fact, I don't even hear her. Many couples are opposite in this regard. You can imagine what this does to communication when one spouse wants to talk and cannot get the attention of the other. What often happens is the one seeking to gain attention gets louder and louder, and the other tunes him out even more or gets annoyed.

This is not a fatal problem once both partners understand it and work on it. We have found that instead of becoming a source of irritation, it can provoke humor. To this day, Bev or the children will react to my lack of attention to their conversations with, "Hi, wall! How are the wife and kids?" If I hear it, we all laugh; if not, I awake from my fog, aware I am the object of their fun.

5. *Unresolved differences produce conflicts.* Most couples find after the honeymoon that they have far more temperament, background, and personal differences than they ever dreamed possible. These differences must be brought out through communication and discussed openly. Eventually, a plan of operation involving change for one, or compromise for both, is essential. Otherwise it will ultimately prove disastrous when such differences produce a clash of wills.

A ridiculous illustration of this occurred during our second year of marriage. We lived in two rooms of a 16-room

Southern mansion while attending college, in exchange for my doing the yard work. One beautiful evening we had a lovely dinner on the patio while the owners were away. It was a delightful setting, but we ruined it. Bev was about three months pregnant with our first child, so I suggested she should drink her milk. (Every prospective father knows unborn babies need the calcium which milk provides.) Bev said, "I don't drink milk." Frankly, I thought that was stupid. I thought everyone drank milk, particularly an expectant mother. So I urged tactfully; she refused. I tried being forceful and threatened; she still refused. Finally I said, "Honey, if you don't drink that milk, I'm going to pour it on your head!" to which she replied, "Then you'd better pour it, because I'm not drinking that milk." You just don't tell a 22-year-old carnal choleric that you're not going to do something! So I stupidly poured it on her head. It destroyed communication at our house for two days, not to mention ruining what could have been a lovely evening. Many years later, all I can think of to describe that scene is the literary gem, "What fools these mortals be!"

Weapons That Destroy Communication

Self-preservation is the well-advertised first law of life— as true psychologically as it is physically. Dr. Henry Brandt says, "There is no nakedness comparable to psychological nakedness." All of us employ weapons to protect ourselves from exposure. The problem with their use is that they stifle communication. Consider them carefully; they are to be avoided.

1. *Explosion.* A very effective tool for self-defense, and the one most commonly used at home, is an angry explosion. This engenders an argumentative spirit and invariably does more damage than good. Explosion teaches a partner that we have a limit on how far we can be pushed, automatically

closing ourselves off to communication in that area. We spent ample time on this in chapter 4, so it does not warrant repetition, except to say that Spirit-controlled family members do not use this tool, or they cease being Spirit-controlled.

2. *Tears.* Next to explosion, and often as a result of it, tears are the most popular psychological weapons we use to defend ourselves. Naturally, tears are more popular with women than with men and are very effective in saying, "If you push me too far, I'll cry." Once the dam breaks into a flood of tears, conversation comes to a screeching halt, unless the attacker is so insensitive that he ruthlessly lashes out in spite of them.

3. *Criticism.* It takes an extremely mature person to accept disagreement, criticism, or opposition without being defensive. The natural inclination (though not a very spiritual reaction) is to criticize the other person. Some forceful types soon learn they can keep their partners off balance and under threat of critical attack, and thus force them to avoid bringing up anything unpleasant or distasteful. This may stifle communication, but it does nothing for love. One dominant, compulsive wife castigated her husband verbally from the time he came in the house until he left. She would rip the newspaper from his hands, constantly telling and retelling whatever bothered her (for as far back as courtship, 35 years before). One day she talked to him endlessly through the bathroom door and finally burst in on him, thinking he wasn't listening. This man used to drive aimlessly around the city in his car, just dreading going home. Talking may be a relief valve to the talker, but it certainly is no relief to the hearer.

4. *Silence.* Phlegmatics and some melancholies have found silence a great tool in avoiding the unpleasant. Whether it is

avoiding an argument by silence (through hiding behind the newspaper or slinking off into the bathroom or garage), it is an aggravating weapon to the one it is used upon. The extroverted temperaments find it all but impossible to use silence as a weapon. Sanguines can't be silent more than 30 seconds at a time, and cholerics are not much better. The weapon of silence usually takes two forms: retreat or resentment.

Those who retreat into a self-protective shell are telling their opponent (or partner) that if they push too hard, they will pull "the turtle act" and pop their head inside a shell, cutting off all communication. Those who use silence out of resentment are really angry people. A phlegmatic man whose slow speech made him no match for his ChlorSan wife (who could talk like a machine gun running wide open) told me, "I've finally discovered how to handle that woman!" When I inquired as to his new technique he replied, "Silence! She can't stand it! Last week I went five days without saying a word to her." I warned him that ultimately that kind of angry resentment would give him ulcers. He laughed and said, "I'm a phlegmatic; they don't get ulcers." Little did either of us dream that in two weeks he would have to be rushed to the hospital with just such a malady, at 28 years of age.

The longest I have known anyone to be silent toward a spouse through anger was 21 days. And, believe it or not, they were both extremely dedicated Christian workers. She was a ChlorSan who made snap judgments, and he was a PhlegMel scholar who was extremely deliberate. She talked throughout nine-tenths of their marriage, made most of the decisions, and outargued him during every debate or discussion. He finally resorted to silence until she would shut up and let him say what was really in his heart. It was incredible to me that two people could be married for 30 years and have to resort to such weapons in order to live together. She had to "study to be quiet," and he had to repent of his anger.

5. *Endless chatter.* Some people can't stand silence. It is almost as though they fear that silence will provide the partner and family with an opportunity to ask some devastating question that might expose their weaknesses. So they talk and talk and talk. I've met people who (I felt certain) must talk in their sleep, because it obviously took no conscious thought to direct their tongues. Consequently, they chatter endlessly about nothing.

Usually this is a sign of an extremely insecure person (although some are like the dominant, compulsive person mentioned under point 3). Such individuals are dreadfully afraid of exposure, unaware they are exposing themselves. Women seem to tend to this loquacious lifestyle more than men, although I have seen my share of male supertalkers also.

The husband of such a talker was meeting with me regularly and had really learned to walk in the Spirit. One day he came in for his appointment with a smile, to tell what he had done the night before. It seemed that his wife had been running off at the mouth for almost an hour when he got up, walked to her side, and gently placed his hand over her mouth and said, "Sweetheart, I love you; I love you; I love you, but my ears need a rest!" They both laughed, and gradually she is learning to slow down her torrent of words.

There are other weapons which people use to stifle true communication, but these are the most common. If you find yourself using them, trust God for victory, that you might enjoy the love and sound mind He wants to give to you and your partner.

Nine Keys to Effective Communication

Like almost everything else, effective communication is an art that must be cultivated by two people. It requires the effort of both the listener and the speaker. The following nine suggestions are keys to better family communication and are designed to ease those special issues that must be dealt with by head-to-head communication.

1. *Learn to understand your partner.* Getting to know another person thoroughly is not a simple feat, and it certainly cannot be done before marriage. Most spouses live together many years before they really understand each other. One of the reasons is that they are both so wrapped up in themselves that they married for the wrong reasons. They had in mind that their partners would understand them.

It is amazing how many people are obsessed with the desire that their partners understand them, when in reality they should be more concerned with understanding their partners. A noted family counselor said, "If your supreme desire is to be understood, you are a sick person." The whole thrust of the gospel is to give as Christ gave to us. One of the basic signs of a selfish person is that he is not interested in understanding and accepting others, but desires that they should accept and understand *him.*

The best tool known for helping you learn to understand your partner is the temperament theory. It explains "actions and reactions" in such a way that it takes the sting out of why your partner acts as he does. Many a source of irritation is resolved when, for example, it becomes apparent that a tendency to talk is a reflection of a sanguine nature, or that a partner's exasperating analytical scrutiny is an outgrowth of his melancholy temperament. Add to this the differences in the sexes, backgrounds, and values, and you will see that it takes a good deal of time to really learn to understand one's partner. When, however, that time of understanding arrives, it removes considerable heat from the relationship when differences come into conflict.

2. *Accept your partner unconditionally and cheerfully.* Everyone fears rejection—some temperaments more than

others. But the more we love someone, the greater is our desire for his or her acceptance. And because we all communicate by expressing emotion as well as by speaking, it is imperative that couples truly accept each other so that they will sincerely emote that acceptance. This is particularly true when difficulties or problem areas in the marriage must be discussed. Like understanding, the assurance of acceptance removes heat from a potentially difficult situation, while the fear of rejection is like pouring gasoline on a fire.

Both of the above steps are basic and should be continually cultivated throughout a marriage, not just at pressure times. When they are, it softens the times when issues and differences must be dealt with head-on.

3. *Plan a suitable time for your partner.* Most communication sessions are instigated by one of the members of the family—usually one of the partners. Some partners are sharp in the morning; they are called "robins." The "owls" are just the opposite; they wake up slowly but are often night people. Obviously, it is best to pick a time that is best suited to your partner. A good rule to follow in this regard is: Never talk about money or "heavy" problems after 9:30 or 10:00 PM. Somehow, all problems look darker and loom larger at night. Learning to understand your partner makes it easier to schedule the best time for a communication session. With most men, it is after dinner when devotions are complete. Sometimes couples have to go out for dinner to assure privacy from the children.

Communication sessions are not limited to the parents; sometimes the teenagers initiate such a session. I recall that one of ours called us into a meeting to point out he did not think the rest of the fancily treated one of his friends properly. Suddenly the reason came out: "Why should we? The guy's a real jerk!" said one of the teens. As you can imagine, we had a lively discussion. The thrust of it was that one young person felt sorry for this neglected kid; his brother and sisters didn't like the friend. As soon as he conveyed his concern for the other teen, we all found it easier to understand his motives and pledged to be more polite to his friend. Such open confrontation is healthy.

4. *Introduce the subject tactfully.* The more difficult the subject, the more tactfully it should be presented. Most couples learn little techniques that after a while signal a "heavy" communication session. Whenever Bev says, "Honey, can I share something with you?" I get a good grip on my fractured ego. I know "it" is coming. When I say to her, "Honey, are you in a good mood tonight?" she turns a little green around the gills and prepares for that moment of truth. Sometimes your partner may not feel up to facing a weakness or problem area. Be prepared to delay the session, remembering you're more interested in maintaining a lasting relationship than in clinging to some particular issue.

5. *Speak the truth in love* (Ephesians 4:15). Lovingly share how you feel and how you assess the situation or the problem or what bugs you. Say it simply, truthfully, but always lovingly. For although love never dilutes the truth, neither does it inflict unnecessary injury. Truth is sharp and it may hurt. For example, when a wife informs her husband she thinks he ought to put his own socks in the hamper or use better table manners, or the husband suggests the wife may be more tolerant with one child than she is with another, or that she has been getting careless with the housework, it will hurt. Truth usually does. But such communication is like surgery—it can't help people without hurting them. Because the surgeon cares about his patients, however, he never makes his incisions greater than necessary.

6. *Allow for reaction time.* It would be ideal if we were all so mature that our response to being confronted with a

serious weakness or flaw in our makeup would be to thank the person who shared the truth. But who is really that ideal? Only the Spirit-controlled man or woman! Most other people will become defensive and react accordingly. Some may resort to one or more of the weapons for self-defense mentioned earlier.

When initiating communication on a sensitive issue, you had better be ready with a calm spirit to take anything your partner offers. For if you react to your spouse's reaction, you have ruined the session. And the responsibility for peace is on you, since you knew in advance what you were going to say and could prepare for it. However, your partner is usually taken by surprise. Actually, you can trust God to be ready with a "soft answer," for as we have seen, it turns away wrath. By giving a soft answer: "We'll think about it," or "I hope I haven't hurt you, but that is how it seemed to me," you can often make your point.

7. *Never argue or defend yourself.* Squelch the desire to defend your position and, unless you are requested to do so, don't give illustrations. If you do, one or two will suffice. Remember, you are sowing a delicate seed into the mind of the one you love. Give it time to germinate.

8. *Pray about it.* Another big asset for Christians is prayer. Not only is it beneficial in getting us to humble ourselves as we get down on our knees before God, but it realistically brings a third party into our relationship. There is no question that families which pray about their problems and differences have much less heat in dealing with them, because they have Someone else vitally involved. When a couple reaches an impasse, both can agree to pray and ask God to help them discern who is right or what course of action should be followed. If they have hurt or insulted one another, after prayer it is a simple thing to apologize and ask forgiveness. Many communication sessions end with the necessity for one

192 ** The Spirit-Filled Family

partner to apologize for violating or not respecting the rights of the other. Next to the three golden words of marriage, "I love you," is the next most important triplet: "I am sorry." Confession to God eases confession to man.

It is amazing to me that so many of the Christian couples who believe in prayer (and believe that all Christian couples ought to pray), often neglect to do so. I once took a survey and found that less than 30 percent prayed three times a week. Every Christian couple should pray regularly. This book will be read by many an individual whose partner is not a Christian or who is so carnal as to refuse to pray. Don't force it. You are not alone; you can "pray to your Father who is in the secret place . . . who . . . will reward you openly" (Matthew 6:6). In fact, once you have communicated a matter to your partner, you have through prayer a court of higher appeals to which you can turn. This does two things: It realistically incurs the blessing of God on your problem, and it helps you to back off once you have stated the issue. This allows your partner to think over your statement. Men are particularly reluctant to admit error, although when filled with the Spirit, they do. It is a wise partner who does not demand verbal agreement, since it is a change of behavior you really desire. By prayer you can in faith anticipate such a change, but it must be instituted by God, not you.

9. *Commit the matter to God.* Once you have communicated on some difficult subject, be it sex, children, finances, mother-in-law, vacation, or the million other problem areas which a marriage and family produce, commit it to God. *Don't nag!* That usually means to discuss it only once. Sometimes you may get by with bringing the same subject up a second time, but it is almost always considered nagging to approach it three times. Because all of us are impatient by nature (some temperaments more than others), it is often difficult to wait for the desired change of behavior we seek. This is again another reason that Christian family living is so much to be

preferred over an ungodly home. We have a heavenly Father to whom we can commit our ways, desires, and needs. Of this you can be certain: God blesses those who commit themselves and their problems to Him.

We have several examples of God's miraculous response to the Christian who commits his problem to Him, once having made it known to his partner. None is more humorous than the lady who wrote to tell us how God worked out a sexual difficulty. The couple had been married 11 years and, although she loved her husband, she had never experienced an orgasm. Like many other women in this modern age, since the wife knew of this possibility, she felt she was being cheated in this area. At a local Christian bookstore she bought *The Act of Marriage*, read it, and suggested her husband do so, but to no avail. She then tactfully precipitated a communication session and clearly informed him that she was "unfulfilled" in this area. Her phlegmatic mate crashed into his shell of self-protection by telling her that "nice girls aren't interested in such things" (as if a man is qualified to know what "nice girls" do in marriage). His wife implored him that the book says that no couple need settle for anything less than mutual satisfaction and again asked him to read the book. He refused. Recognizing that if she brought it up again it would be nagging, and seeking to be a woman of God, she prayed about it and committed it to Him.

Her letter then told us what happened. Her husband was invited to a men's luncheon in a Midwestern city where I spoke to a group of men and concluded with a question-and-answer period. A man asked the rather hostile question, "Pastor LaHaye, why did you, a minister, write such a book as *The Act of Marriage?*" It got deathly quiet for a moment so I replied, "For these reasons: First, too many Christian wives have the misconception that lovemaking is evil or ugly. I felt it was time they heard a minister give the biblical perspective that God meant it to be good and beautiful. And second, too many Christian men are so uninformed on the subject that they are cheating their wife and themselves out of a lifetime of happiness." The writer then went on to report that her husband came home from work the next evening and rather sheepishly asked, "Where is that marriage book you asked me to read?" He read it and, in a matter of days, their love life was transformed. William Cowper said, "God moves in mysterious ways, His wonders to perform."

Knowing and Accepting

There is no subject a married couple should be unable to discuss *sometime.* It should always be done lovingly and honestly, then committed to God and the partner for whatever change is required. Ignoring difficult subjects or sensitive areas solves nothing and compounds the problem. Dr. Howard Hendricks has sagely said, "A happy marriage requires two elements: 1) two people who know each other thoroughly (that involves more than knowing a person sexually, although that is included), and 2) two people who accept each other completely." It is likely that no young couple meets those two qualifications completely, for it takes several years of living with a person and hundreds of hours of communication to know your partner thoroughly and to be so Spirit-controlled that you love and accept each other completely. When you do, you have the ideal relationship. If you don't have that kind of relationship at present, you should pray and work for it. You will find it is more than worth the effort.

Chapter 10

Finances and the Home

The love of money may be the root of all evil, but the *misuse* of money is the beginning of many of life's problems. This can be true for single as well as married people. The fast-talking, high-pressure salesman sooner or later reaches inside the home of every American family, or the vast number of catalogs selling everything you would ever need is delivered "right to your home."

One college girl called long distance from her dorm to tell her parents about the wonderful opportunity that had just been offered. A company that has had a history of entrapping young women with an "outstanding offer at a reduced student interest rate" had just swept across her campus. She had fallen for their high-pitched sales talk and believed she could not be happy without their merchandise. She excitedly told about paying "only one dollar a week for six months, then two dollars a week for two years, and twenty-five dollars a month after graduation until it was paid off" (which seemed to be rather an indefinite period). After the interest rate was added, plus the years of payments, they figured out that she was being charged double the price. Her parents finally concluded that if this taught her a valuable lifetime lesson about credit, then it would be worth the extra money she would have to pay. Like so many other "buy now, pay later" contracts, the payments would still be going on long after the thrill and worth of the purchases were over. If she had been forced to pay cash, there would have been no question about her ability to purchase the item, but when she was told that the payments would only be "one or two dollars per week," she concluded that was certainly within her reach.

Recently there have been TV ads that offer "no payments for six months and no interest for one year." All couples need to remind themselves that there is no free lunch. Someday the banker must be paid, and usually with exorbitant interest.

This type of advertising and buying propaganda causes much of the turmoil in American homes today. Buying on credit encourages people to make purchases they cannot afford and perhaps do not need. It has put a new emphasis on possession of material things that is unhealthy and produces an indifferent attitude toward the cost of purchases made. The "good life" is represented to young couples as a quick accumulation on credit of a house full of furniture and other possessions that would normally take 10 to 15 years of marriage to obtain. Many couples within the first few years have surrounded and encumbered their lives with credit from all directions. This "buying power," like a contagious disease, creeps on month after month.

The basic problem in over 70 percent of the marriages that fail stems from finances. When you compound the normal conflicts and disagreements in a home with the financial pressures from overspending and credit-buying, the end results can be hostility, bitterness, and in severe cases, divorce. The insidious enemy in many of these marriages has undoubtedly been credit and the you-can't-live-without-them credit cards. In the earliest stages of marriage, couples rush out to apply for credit so they can become established, only to find later on that credit was their worst enemy and that whatever they had established was now beginning to crumble. Credit buying encourages "impulse" purchasing, giving extra-lavish gifts, plus excessive spending simply because you can take home the merchandise without laying down the cash. Finally, the day of reckoning comes when all the charge slips are totaled and the end-of-the-month statements begin to roll in. Tension mounts, irritability sets in, and tempers flare. What started out to be a normal way of living suddenly turns into a hotbed of frustration and accusations.

How Financial Pressures Reveal Themselves

1. *Excessive shopping.* Financial pressures bring on a depressed spirit, and some people experience a temporary relief from depression by purchasing more new items. Of course, in the end this only compounds the already-existing problem.

2. *Critical spirit.* A woman is especially guilty of criticizing when under pressure. She will begin to pick at and nag about everything the husband does that does not quite suit her, even to the point of blowing small things out of proportion. This gives her an escape valve to let off some of the inner pressure that has been building up.

3. *Lying and deceit.* The most common and complex way to hide money matters is by lying. Both husbands and wives are often guilty of financial deceit in order to satisfy their material impulses. When money is spent lavishly or foolishly, they discover the need to lie in order to get out of a difficult financial situation and their own embarrassment.

4. *Seeking self-pity.* This person talks about the financial problems over and over again, in the hope that others will

feel sorry for him and provide temporary comfort. If there is no obvious effort for self-help, sympathy will do more harm than good.

5. *Extreme fatigue.* It may come on very slowly, until the person cannot remember when he began to feel so tired. Living with irritation and accusations causes one to feel defeated before he ever begins.

6. *Psychological illnesses.* Tensions and stress over a long period of time are the greatest contributors toward self-induced illnesses. Anyone living under the pressure of final notices or collectors' calls is certainly a ripe candidate for this problem.

7. *Angry accusations.* Accusations of stupidity, indifference, in-law interference, and selfishness are a few of the darts that are thrown back and forth. It is easier to blame the other partner for the financial mess in the family than to accept much of the problem as one's own and set forth to correct it.

8. *Temporary frigidity.* It is very difficult to continue a close sexual relationship when tension is mounting and resentments are building. If this condition continues for a long period of time, the temporary frigidity can grow and develop into a sexual hopelessness for that marriage. One husband said that he felt as if he were paying to have intercourse with his wife since she only engaged in lovemaking when the money flowed freely.

9. *Silent treatment.* When the sexual relationship comes to a halt, it is not long before communication ceases—at least *normal* communication. There may be screaming and yelling from one side, while the other partner clams up and remains silent. The silent one is usually filled with resentment

toward the other partner. The more one spouse is silent, the more the other screams, until conditions move from bad to worse.

10. *Finally, separation.* In the midst of despair, many couples falsely believe that they can better work out their problems if they separate. At this point in the marriage, most couples are not able to think too soundly and therefore are willing to escape reality and run from the financial mess they are in. Before couples reach this point, they should follow the wise advice given in Proverbs 12:15: "The way of a fool is right in his own eyes, but he who heeds counsel is wise."

It seems that the money problem in marriage relationships is the last one about which a couple will seek counsel. When couples face sexual difficulties, turmoil with children, and so on, they are more willing to find help than when they face financial disaster. Men especially feel that this is a reflection on their male superiority, and ego keeps them from seeking help. Too often they wait until it is too late and the damage has already been done. The Bible says that a wise man is one who takes heed of counsel.

Money Is in God's Plan

Money is necessary and a part of God's plan for His people. It is only the love of money and its misuse that are destructive. The Bible has much instruction for us on how to manage our money. Therefore, we must conclude that how we handle it is a part of our Christian walk.

We recommend to all young couples that they talk over and develop a single budget, so both husband and wife are well aware of where their money is going. Many couples have found this to be a real eye-opener and a tremendous help in solving the money pressures they have created (or even before they are created). The main purpose of a budget is to identify and put controls on excessive and miscellaneous spending. Don't scoff at a budget! If you are already in debt, then you desperately need one to help you balance your spending with your income. Proverbs 16:9 says, "A man's heart plans his way, but the LORD directs his steps." The first step of planning is a simple, useful budget.

You cannot plan a budget and expect God to direct your steps until you are willing to honor Him with the firstfruits of your income. In other words, obey God and be sure that tithing is in your budget plan. "'Bring all the tithes into the storehouse, that there may be food in My house, and prove Me now in this', says the LORD of hosts, 'if I will not open for you the windows of heaven and pour out for you such blessing that there will not be room enough to receive it'" (Malachi 3:10). Now *there* is a promise that you cannot afford to pass up! The Lord says to test Him by giving the whole tithe to Him, and He will bless you until there is no more need. It sounds impossible, but remember that our God deals in the impossible things of life, and He challenges you to test Him.

During our first year of marriage, we were both students in college, and money was very tight. Tim was a GI, and his tuition was covered by veterans' benefits. The amount allotted us for living expenses was 120 dollars per month, which had to cover tithe, rent, food, transportation, clothing, and my college tuition. There was no way it could stretch that far, and we consistently ran behind. We also pastored a little country church 35 miles away on weekends. This offered 15 dollars a week, barely enough to cover the travel expenses. We were very happy in our first church and trusted God to work out our impossible financial situation. At one point, my college tuition was due, and we did not have the money to cover it. In fact, between us we had 50 cents to last two weeks. Again we trusted God to help us through the next two weeks by stretching that 50 cents, and we committed my tuition bill to Him. The next day Tim went to our mailbox and found a check to cover the tuition exactly. Various states paid veterans a bonus, and the state of Michigan was the first to pay. During those days we tithed very scrupulously every bit of income we received. God passed the test, as far as we were concerned. Now, many married years later, we can honestly say God has been extremely faithful to us, and we have tithed (and more) every cent that we have received. In fact, He has done "exceedingly abundantly above all that we ask or think" (Ephesians 3:20).

Several years ago, Tim challenged the members of our congregation to step out by faith and raise their tithe for the year to 20 percent. It was called "double tithing" and was a real act of faith for the many families who committed themselves to this increased giving. At the close of the year, we spoke with several of the families to see if any had continued this 20-percent giving for the entire year. Our hearts were thrilled as we heard family after family testify of God's great faithfulness to them. Over and over we heard stories about how God had stretched their 80 percent further than they could have stretched the full 100 percent. Not one of these families experienced financial hardship for that year. We should not have been surprised, because, after all, that is exactly what He promised to do. But even now as I record this story on paper, my heart is filled to overflowing when I think that God in His great faithfulness will never disappoint us when He makes a promise to us.

This experience occurred during one of the most serious recessions we'd ever had in our city, and unemployment was extremely high. While attending a ministers' meeting, Tim heard a local pastor comment on how many men in his congregation were out of work, so he inquired as to the size of the pastor's congregation. When Tim returned to the office, he counted the number of our own members who were unemployed and, comparing the size of our congregation with the other pastor's, found that our unemployment level was 18 times lower than that of the other church. Several men reported during those days that others in their departments were laid off during serious cutbacks, but for some "mysterious" reason our men seemed to be supernaturally protected. You cannot outgive the Lord!

The minimum tithe is usually considered to be ten percent. However, the Old Testament required 23 1/3 percent. If a man gave less, he was robbing God. Each couple must determine what percentage to give, keeping in mind the biblical principle: "He who sows sparingly will also reap sparingly, and he who sows bountifully will also reap bountifully. So let each one give as he purposes in his heart, not grudgingly or of necessity; for God loves a cheerful giver" (2 Corinthians 9:6,7).

Mortgage Payments

In today's inflationary economy, it is utterly impossible for a young couple to own a house and car without mortgage payments. The safeguard for purchasing a car would be to make sure that the down payment is high enough so that the amount owed is not greater than the resale value of the car. Don't be bitten by the "car bug" that makes you discontent with an older car. In 1976, as we traveled to 46 foreign countries to minister to missionaries, we found many American-made cars being driven with well over 300,000 (and even 400,000) miles on them. In America we have been led to believe that after 100,000 miles there isn't much good left in a car. Precaution should be taken not to attempt buying a home and a new car in the same year. This could be financial suicide. When you take on a mortgage, either for a home or a car, the debt begins on the date the monthly payment is due. Be certain that the payments are low enough so that you can pay them as scheduled. Before going into debt for a house or car, carefully examine your other expenditures to be sure they are trimmed down to enable you to take on another monthly payment.

We are instructed in Psalms: "The wicked borrows and does not repay, but the righteous shows mercy and gives" (37:21). Proverbs 22:7 states: "The rich rules over the poor, and the borrower is servant to the lender." It reminds us very strongly that God wants us to have financial freedom regardless of what our income might be.

Some teach it is wrong to go into debt even for a home or car. We consider them both necessities and feel a young family will rarely be able to start out paying cash for either. We think it is permissible, even necessary, for most couples starting out to raise enough of the down payment so the value of the house or car is always more than the total debt. Never mortgage more for a home than you can afford.

To enable you to trim down any excessive spending, here are a few basic questions that should be asked before each purchase that is not considered an absolute necessity for survival:

1. Do we need the item?
2. Do we have the money to pay cash (or to not exceed our credit capability)?
3. Is it high on our priority list?
4. Did we pray about it?
5. Have we shopped for the best buy?

If all these questions can be answered in the affirmative, then ask one more:

6. Did we ask God to either confirm or remove the desire for it?

If the answer is still yes, then proceed wisely. If answers are negative, then thank God for keeping you from making an unwise purchase.

Avoiding Financial Crises

There are many books available to help families plan a simple and workable budget. You may have one that works for your financial situation, but if not, we have provided one that could get you started in the right direction. For financial success, it is best to plan ahead before you hit a financial crisis, and that can be accomplished with a budget.

At this present time, the national figures indicate that the average income for a family of four is between $35,000 and $40,000 annually with one working parent. For an example of a workable budget, we will use the middle figure of approximately $37,500 annual gross salary for a family of four. Any extra income that the wife could earn by home projects would be over and above what we have figured. Do not use the extra income that the wife earns for the regular operating budget. Let her assistance provide for the children's education, vacations, emergency medical expenses, etc. You may decide that it is necessary to alter the percentages on one or two of the items due to variations in your locale, but the total must not exceed 100 percent. All amounts are rounded to the nearest dollar.

Taxes are always on the gross income, and at the present time taxes are approximately 24 percent at this salary range.

	Annual	Monthly
Gross income	$37,500	$3,125
* Taxes at 24 %	9,000	750
Net salary income	$28,500	$2,375
Tithe at 10 %	2,850	238
	$25,650	$2,137

*State and federal taxes may vary slightly from year to year. The balance after 24% for taxes and 10% for tithing will be divided into monthly expenses.

Expenses	%	Annual	Monthly
Housing (payments, property taxes, insurance, utilities)	36	$9,234	$770
Automobile (payments, gas, oil, repairs, insurance, license)	13	$3,335	$278
Food (not junk food or restaurants)	26	$6,669	$556
Insurance (life, health, disability)	6	$1,539	$128
Clothing (Shop wisely.)	6	$1,539	$128
Debts (This is the item most needing careful surveillance.)	5	$1,282	$107
Miscellaneous (entertainment, recreation, vacation)	3	$770	$64
Medical, dental, prescriptions (This is assuming average health and that you have group medical insurance. If you do not, it may be necessary to trim the car, clothing, and/or miscellaneous allowances.)	5	$1,282	$106
Savings (If you have had a year without many medical bills, auto repairs, and so on, save any excess. This will enable you to be a cash buyer and eventually eliminate the 5% for debts and rid yourself of credit cards.)	?	?	?
Total	100	$25,650	$2,137

The above is just a suggested shell of a budget. It will not succeed exactly as is for you; you must work at it. If you have been deeply in debt, do not expect a budget to solve your problems overnight. It will take much sacrifice and self-denial to put your financial house in order. But remember: With God's help it can be done. The peace of mind and the order that is restored to your home will be well worth all the denials and limits you put on your spending.

Who Should Handle the Money?

This question should be openly discussed before the marriage begins, so each partner knows how the other feels about the subject. There is no absolute answer to this question. However, after counseling many couples in the midst of their conflicts, we have come to believe that it is important in the first few years of married life that the husband handles the finances. During this time, the new bride should be adjusting to a spirit of submission and teamwork. If she is handling the money, this is one area in which she does not have to learn to submit because she is in control. Usually it can be said that the one who handles the money controls the family, particularly in the first few years.

After the wife has adjusted to her new husband's role as head of the house, if they are both in full agreement, she could take over the family bookkeeping. Even then, it must be a team effort. The family income belongs to both of them, and together they should plan and agree on how it should be spent. There should be no money secrets between them if they are going to have harmony in their marriage.

Each partner should be allowed an equal amount of money to be used as personal spending money. The amount is not the important factor. A person can adjust to varying amounts. It may be used for gifts for other people or for one's own personal needs. The important thing is that it is a fund, however small, that is used any way one chooses. In the suggested budget on the previous page, it would come under "miscellaneous."

Some couples have agreed on splitting the responsibility of bookkeeping. The husband deposits the paycheck in his account and then writes a check to his wife to deposit in her household and personal checkbook. Here would be the budgeted amount for food, clothing for the family, sundries, and her own personal fund. The husband keeps in his checkbook the balance to cover tithe, taxes, house and auto payments, insurance, debts, and so on, plus his own personal fund that is equal to his wife's.

It is important for the husband to keep in mind that a woman does not like to ask for every dollar she receives. Too often a husband will hold such a tight grip on his wallet that it creates a spirit of bitterness and resentment in his wife. Finally, in exasperation, she explodes and he wonders, "What in the world is wrong with her?" She spends an equal time keeping the family together and the household functioning well. Does she not deserve an equal say in how the money should be handled? Much contention can be avoided if the husband handles the main checkbook and the couple budget a regular amount the wife can count on each month to cover household and the wife's personal expenses. More on that later.

Working Wives

This heading may be misleading because it implies that some wives work and others do not. Every wife who is worth anything will be a "working" wife. However, some will work in the home, others outside, and there will be those who must do both, at least for a while.

In today's economy, most young wives find it advantageous to work for a few years before they start a family. This is especially true if they still have college loans to pay off. In many cases it becomes necessary in order for a young couple to handle the high cost of rent, food, and transportation. However, it is wise for couples to adjust as quickly as possible to living on only the husband's income. The wife's salary should be "extra" money that is allowed to accumulate for a down payment on a home, or perhaps used to pay off college debts. Whatever the "extra" may be, care should be taken not to depend on the second income for living expenses. Unfortunately, all too often the couple enjoys the luxury of two incomes and may postpone buying a home and starting a family. It is at this strategic time that some couples selfishly decide that having a family is too costly, so they head toward a childless future.

If the wife continues to work after the children come, there are more complications to face. There will be the need for baby-sitters who will spend more time with the children during their waking hours than the mother will. Likewise, the mother will spend the best hours of her day—when she is most alert, patient, kind, responsive, and ambitious—away from her children. The couple needs to analyze the wife's wages against the additional expenses that working generates. In addition, both need to consider the federal, state, and Social Security taxes, plus tithe. Some of the common expenses that must come out of the remainder would be baby-sitting fees, additional meals in restaurants, noneconomical fast meals at home, transportation to and from work, parking fees, increased wardrobe, and perhaps extra help in the home.

It might prove to be better economically if the wife stayed at home, saved on baby-sitting fees, planned delicious, low-cost, home-cooked meals, plus cut the additional expenses and considered a part-time job that she could do at home. I have discovered several ways that women can earn extra money at home, and I am sure there are many more. A few such jobs would be typing labels, stuffing envelopes, baby-sitting for someone else, teaching piano lessons (if qualified), editing and printing term papers for local college students, typing manuscripts, or doing neighborhood sewing. The home computer, fax machine, and printer have enabled 40 million people to work out of their homes today, making this the fastest-growing industry in the country. When their children enter school, some women have been able to find employment where the hours of work coincided with school hours. This allows the mothers to be home when the children arrive. The creative woman will find a way to make the budget stretch and still be able to raise her own children. I feel that it is extremely important for a mother not to work away from home while she still has preschool children. The first few years of life are the most important, and no one is going to be as concerned and diligent in the children's training as their own parent.

There are more and more parents who feel the urgent need to give their elementary and high-school children a Christian education. It does cost additional money which may not be in the budget. In some cases, mothers whose children are in private school may consider getting a job during those hours to pay the cost of a Christian education. Because of the moral and philosophical problems caused by many public schools, a Christian education—either in private school or through home schooling—is gaining an increasingly higher priority with many Christian parents.

May I suggest that the Christian community be careful to examine the financial arrangements of their pastors and pastors' families. In years past, ministers have been underpaid, and many wives were forced to go to work just to keep body and soul together. As Christian women saw the wife of the pastor going outside the home to work, they followed her example, and it was not always an absolute necessity for them. Consequently, children have been and are being raised in day-care centers or by local baby-sitters because church leaders presented this example to their congregations without considering the consequences.

We recognize that there are situations today where mothers have no choice but to work outside the home. There may have been the death of the husband, a divorce, or a separation. What a wonderful chance this is for another mother, who may need to work herself, to become a daytime substitute mother (or baby-sitter) to help raise these children in love and good training. Both families can benefit from such an act of Christian grace. In fact, I met a sharp young mother who wanted to raise her own baby while her husband was finishing medical school, so she set up a day-care center in her home. She netted more income each month than she did working in her profession, and she got to stay home and do it.

Another danger for working wives must be mentioned. When a wife gets a job working outside the home for an employer, she has to meet certain qualifications. For example, she must be neat and attractive; she must submit to the employer's authority while at the office; she must be polite and appreciative, alert and productive, and flexible in maintaining a work schedule in keeping with the employer's plans. These are all examples of a businesswoman, but are also good characteristics of an ideal wife. It is possible for these interests and concerns to be confused and compared to the partner at home. The feeling can develop that the "male coworker" at the office is more attractive, efficient, and capable than the one at home, and this is an attitude that must be squelched at the very start.

A Christian Should Have a Will

Good stewardship involves making a will that not only provides for your loved ones, but also designates a percentage or a tithe of your estate to be given to a Christian organization of your choice. What a lasting testimony it can be when, after your death, your money continues on in the Lord's work. We have both been involved with our own ministries—Beverly with Concerned Women for America, and Tim with Family Life Seminars. It has been our suggestion that when Christians are making a will, they consider leaving a tithe, or more, of their estate to a Christian ministry. Several have chosen to do this for our ministries over the years because they wanted to have a continuing effect on the nation for their children and grandchildren. It is interesting that many times this comes as a total surprise to people who have never considered the idea before. These people are all Christians and good stewards of their money while living. But the thrill comes in knowing that, even after their death, they can be faithful in distributing their money as the Bible instructs.

If a person dies without a will, the state will dispose of his property according to state law, and that could impose hardships and restrictions on the family left behind. Consult with a lawyer who can write the will and perhaps set up a living trust for you at a reasonable fee. The day will surely come when it will be worth all the planning devoted to disposing of your earthly possessions.

Before we left on the nine-month around-the-world missionary trip we mentioned earlier, we were advised to update our will. Now that was a startling thought at first because we had every intention of returning home. But we followed this good advice and met with our lawyer to finalize the papers. Just a few days before we left the country, we called our four children and the two married partners to our home for the evening. It was our plan to share with them what we had done and to inform them of the percentages we requested be left to specific Christian organizations. We did not want it to be a surprise to them. It was a time of heavy, serious talk, and then we had prayer together. What a joy it was to let them in on our burden for these organizations and hear them share it also as they joined us in prayer for each one. That will was accomplishing much in the lives of our own children even before our death.

An important part of the Christian life is the discipline of keeping one's financial house in proper order. "Let all things be done decently and in order" (1 Corinthians 14:40).

Since this book was originally written, Tim has teamed up with a financial consultant, Jerry Tuma of Dallas, and his wife, Mona, an excellent women's Bible teacher. They have enthusiastically supported the temperament teaching for years. Together they wrote *Smart Money*, a book that shows how your temperament influences the way you spend your money, and what to do about it. It is available in most

Christian bookstores or can be ordered from:

Family Life Seminars
370 L'Enfant Promenade, S.W. # 801
Washington, D.C. 20024

Chapter 11

How to Raise Good Children in a Hostile Culture

The most family-friendly culture in the history of man was that of America from the colonial days until around the turn of the century. The reason was that this country was founded by Christians for the purpose of religious freedom. They built this nation on Judeo-Christian principles which they brought with them from northern Europe where they had been persecuted for their Christian faith, largely by the established state churches. In fact, those biblical principles are the secret to the greatness of America. That period lasted about 300 years, from 1620 to almost 1930.

Then came the period when the secularizers of education, the entertainment industry, and the media (mostly newspapers in those days) began to elect predominately secular-minded politicians to run the government. Together they gained virtual control of our society and culture. Prior to that, the churches were the most dominant influence on society. In our book *A Nation Without a Conscience*, we show how the church ceased to be the molder of our nation's conscience around 1930. Today that conscience is primarily set by the entertainment industry based in Hollywood and on

Broadway—hardly bastions of religious beliefs and moral principles. If anything, Hollywood, much of education, and the media are hostile to moral values. The morally depraved programming currently beamed into the American home in the name of entertainment would have been against the law just 30 years ago. The liberal politicians who have been elected and promoted to run the government during the past 40 or more years have passed laws that are directly opposed to the good of the nation's families—from overtaxation to pay for the "welfare state" philosophy, which has nearly bankrupt the nation and destroyed many of the families who receive it, to creating an obsession with sex through teaching explicit sex education for 30 years while refusing to teach abstinence (because it is too religious). Now government supports giving out condoms to eighth-grade children in some districts, while still refusing to teach virtue and abstinence.

Secularism Is Called "Foolishness" in the Bible

As these liberal leaders forced secularism on this nation, America has turned from her religious roots and adopted the "anything goes" values of secular humanism. Consequently, our citizens have lost freedom, integrity, morality, and even safety in our streets. We have liberal judges who show more concern for violent criminals than they do for their victims; consequently, we have become the crime capital of the world. Nothing that liberal secularizers promise turns out the way they forecast. I remember when the extremely liberal president Lyndon Johnson launched the "Great Society" that was supposed to solve poverty in our country. Since then we have wasted over five trillion dollars on welfare and have more people on the dole today than when we started—while almost 400 billion dollars a year is spent on just the interest to pay for that 30-year experiment in welfarism which has proven to be a colossal failure. And as tragic as that is for the younger generation who are inheriting a bankrupt America, it is even worse for families when 66 percent of inner-city babies are born without fathers because welfare has subsidized illegitimacy by paying single mothers higher payments than married couples by increasing the amount paid for every baby. Our government has made having babies out of wedlock profitable.

All our nation's major social problems can be laid at the door of the liberal secular humanists who control our society. They have no time for God, His moral principles, or religious values. Liberals are still committed to the old discredited thinking of the Greek humanists who taught, "Man is the measure of all things," while the Bible teaches that God is the measure of all things by pointing out "In the beginning God." They call biblical or religious thinking "foolishness"; God calls their thinking "foolishness" when Scripture states, "Has not God made foolish the wisdom of this world?" (1 Corinthians 1:20). "Man's wisdom" today takes the form of liberal secularism that, as we have seen, dominates four of the most powerful institutions of our society. Education has trained our media and entertainment industry and, until 1994, has elected a brand of liberal politician to carry out "foolish" theories. All these theories have done is produce social chaos and cultural destruction at the expense of the family and hung immense national debt on the necks of the next generation.

Today, instead of government and culture being supportive of the values of the family, they are the enemies of family life. If we are ever to see family-friendly values reestablished in this country, religious-minded citizens will have to go to the polls in unprecedented numbers as they did in 1994 (when 55 percent of Evangelicals voted) and elect only those politicians who support traditional Judeo-Christian values. For only they can break the dictatorial power over education now held by liberal secular humanists who are determined to mold society and its policies after their "foolish thinking" that man can solve the problems of man independent of God. It has never happened in the history of the world, and it won't happen today. If the secularizers who have controlled this country for over 40 years continue to dominate, our nation will be in civil chaos by the year 2000 or shortly thereafter.

If, however, more conservative leaders continue to be elected to office in future elections, we will see this nation once again return to its roots of "one nation under God"— that respects human life (even the unborn and the elderly) and holds all its citizens, regardless of race, creed, or color, accountable for their actions. Then safety will return to our streets and civil sanity will return to our culture. At the point of this writing, there is no way of knowing how the future will play out. I do know there will be a vicious war between liberals and conservatives—led by the media, the entertainment industry, and educators—to regain control of the American mind and, through it, the ballot box. However, if more conservative senators, congressmen, and governors, along with a president are elected in 1996, 1998, and 2000, that chaos may well be averted and laws supportive of family values will be reinstated. If liberals ever regain control of the government, I believe it will be all but over for the preservation of America and her families as we have known them. The loss of religious freedom will soon follow. For liberals will redefine the family, acknowledge homosexual marriages, and promote the welfare state, socialized medicine, and big government. To support it all, they will tax the country into a depression.

The next five years are as important to America as were the years prior to the Civil War or the Revolutionary War. The years 1995- to 2000 will go down in history as the years that America either won or lost the Second American Revolution. For we are in a very important philosophical war between liberal and conservative (or secularist versus religious) thought. Will the twenty-first century be controlled by the now-failed policies of liberalism, or will a limited government of conservative ideas (that recognizes religious values are essential to a morally sane society) prevail? That all depends on the continued growth of conservative means of communicating with the American people and the increased participation of Christians in the voting process.

In the Meantime, You Have a Family to Raise

Cultural change takes place very slowly. Even under the best conditions, all the harmful effects of liberal humanist policies of the past half century will take at least one to two decades to undo. In the meantime, you have a family to raise to love and serve God. To do so, you will have to work hard at insulating your family from the harmful effects that the humanistic attacks on the family have created. The following diagram, taken from the manual I use in conducting Family Life Seminars, shows the extent of the current problem. It

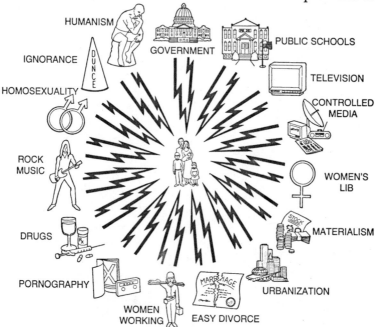

illustrates the 15 hostile forces of humanism as they attack the family. Each is described in detail in my book *The Battle for the Family*.

It is our sincere prayer that no young person will be discouraged from getting married, and that no young couple will decide against raising children because of the hostile culture they will be forced to raise them in. Let's face it, the first-century Christians didn't have it so good either, yet they raised children who conquered the Roman Empire in three centuries. What we are really saying is that you must work harder at protecting the minds and emotions of your children than even your parents did to be equally as successful in childraising. But the good news is, if you will set a high priority of raising good children in this hostile culture and are willing to spend the priority time it takes to do so, you still can be very successful. The following rings of insulation will help you. Some have already been covered in earlier chapters, and some bear repeating from a slightly different point of view. But you, the parents, are the key to protecting your family. We will locate the insulating rings from the outside in. You can arrange them any way you like, but the success you have in raising your children will be in direct proportion to how many rings you use to protect the minds and moral values of your children.

Make Your Home a Haven of Love

The first ring of insulation against the external attacks visualized above is family love. From earliest days, children need to learn they are loved. We have touched on this earlier, but it bears repeating because it is so important. They not only gain a sense of self-worth from being loved by their parents, but it protects them from the fiery darts of the evil one and his emissaries in society by giving them the assurance that home is where they can always find love.

Such love takes time—sometimes sacrificial time. That is why we teach at our seminars that after-dinner/early evening time does not belong to TV—it belongs to the family. That is when parents get in their best expressions of love. From earliest childhood, those few hours each day need to be spent expressing love for the children. A recent survey indicated that the average parent spends less than 30 minutes a day with his or her children. You cannot adequately express love without spending time. Fathers who take time each evening when they are home to read stories to their children not only produce good readers later on, but also children who know they are loved.

As the children mature, they do their own reading, but a close relationship can be nurtured through an ongoing interest in their schoolwork. Children don't care if you're the president of the bank or the head of a department of a college. Their interests are kindergarten, eighth grade, Little League, etc. As much as possible, show your love by involving yourself in their world. You will have plenty of time later for personal growth and development. They may not remember the details, but your children will never forget that their parents made time for them because they loved them.

I have never forgotten when I was eight years old and my father tried to teach me how to ice-skate. He wanted me to be a hockey player. I have the height, coordination, and disposition for it. The problem was, my dad only had one leg. He had his leg amputated four inches below the knee as a result of getting it mashed by a streetcar when he was six years old. But he never let it hold him back. He wore a wooden leg, and most of his friends never knew he was "handicapped." That day his handicap became painfully apparent. After strapping on our skates, he gave me instructions, and we were doing well until suddenly the bolt at the ankle of his wooden leg came apart. His skate and shoe shot across the ice, and he plopped down hard. I gathered up the pieces, and we laughed as he screwed it back together. Finally, he decided that ice-skating was not for one-legged men. One year later he was dead.

Often I have remembered that event when my father, who knew he had no business ice-skating, proved without words how much he loved me. Needless to say, it is a very special memory! His love and my mother's lasting love in raising three children as a single mom have contributed greatly to my strong sense of self-confidence and self-acceptance, even though I only have average natural skills. Why? Because I was loved by the two most important people in my life.

The interesting thing about parental love is that any parent can give it. From the poorest family to the richest, all parents—with Gods' help—can give love. And as we have already seen, the child that receives unconditional love from his parents receives the most important gift in life, next to life itself and salvation through the Giver of love. You who are reading this book and weep because you are so poor that you "can't give much to your children"—take heart! Love is all my godly mother had to give the three of her children—one of whom I was privileged to be. We adored her and, now that she is in heaven, we all revere her memory. We look back on our childhood and think we were rich. And we were. We were loved.

Filter Out the Bad Effects of Our Liberal Culture

I dream of the day when TV and radio will not be permitted to carry programming that is illegal or immoral according to community standards. It wouldn't take an "act of Congress"; all it requires is for the Federal Communications Commission to do what it was originally established for: to simply refuse to renew the broadcasting license of any station that aired illegal violence or other activity that violates acceptable community moral values. Such an action would send a shock wave throughout the industry that would force it to clean itself up in weeks. But that would take the election of several conservative presidents who would appoint FCC members who shared their standards, instead of those who control it now.

In the meantime, Christian parents are going to have to give better surveillance to programming and use Christian TV and radio wherever possible. Fortunately, as we have seen, videos and recordings acceptable to Christians are available in most Christian bookstores. Make sure you use Christian programming rather than permit people who do not share your values to select the programming that goes into the eyes and ears of your children.

Teach Moral Principles for Living

When I was in the ninth grade our "coach," the favorite teacher in our school, was offended because one of the boys used a filthy word in the locker room (the same word is used on TV and in movies today on a regular basis). This coach, a Roman Catholic father of seven children, ordered us up on the gym floor while he preached to us for the entire period on "morality, rights, wrongs, virtue, responsibility, and respect for the opposite sex." It was a great speech—the best sex education lecture I ever received. Yet if that good man were to do such a thing today in the average public school, he would be fired. Not because the parents wouldn't approve—the vast majority even today would thank him. But those who control the so-called "education system" that does such a poor job educating most children, don't believe in the very things our coach tried to instill in us. Obviously, morally sane parents who pay for education through their taxes no longer control our schools. Instead, they are controlled by liberal secular humanists who believe "there are no absolutes," or "one person's morality is as good as another's"—AIDS notwithstanding.

Obviously, if public school students are going to learn moral principles for living, they will have to be taught in the home. Some courageous individual teachers who still believe in the traditional values our country was founded on, including those my coach taught us, are still in the system. Not nearly enough however! All too many advocate an "anything goes" sexual lifestyle—just as long as kids "use a condom." Some teachers even advocate homosexuality as "an optional lifestyle." Such false notions must be counteracted by parents in the home. The church still communicates basic morality, but that is not enough. We in the church only have children's minds two to four hours a week. Public educators have them 35 hours a week. Parents must do a better job teaching biblical values to their children in the home.

If you think we are exaggerating the problem, consider what most youth workers confirm, that the church is losing 35 percent to 50 percent of our youth to the world before they graduate from high school. The reason? In our opinion, it is the 12,000 hours of secular humanist indoctrination they receive in public education from kindergarten through twelfth grade, contrasted with two to four hours a week in church. That must be supplemented in the home. If you want your children to have your moral values, you must teach them yourself. It is the parents' responsibility! Fortunately, there are materials in Christian bookstores that will help you. Bill Gothard has an excellent teaching guide for parents, and William Bennett's bestselling *Book of Virtues* and other helps are available. Check with your youth pastor or Sunday school superintendent. The important thing is, you as the parent should assume the responsibility of teaching moral values to your children.

Provide Your Children with a Pro-moral Local Government

The moral values of your community are set by its leaders, not its people. For too long, Christians and other religious and morally minded citizens have ignored school board, city council, county supervisor, and other statewide elections, not realizing that those people decide what is legal in their community. Consequently, more than 4000 babies are murdered every day, not because it is moral but because it is "legal." Pornography that destroys decency in the mind is also "legal," even though it had been illegal for over 300 years and is a moral blight to any society.

Just as Christians and others are waking up to the necessity to get involved at election time on a national level, so they are beginning to get involved locally. No longer do party affiliations set the criteria by which a politician receives our vote. It is what he or she stands for morally that counts, for the people who set our laws ultimately establish "community standards." If they are set too low, then the ballot box is our resource. We believe every parent has a responsibility to his children, his God, and his neighborhood to be a participating citizen by registering to vote, becoming informed of the values of the candidates, and going to the polls on election day. In addition, many people are circulating the voting records on moral issues of incumbents so that they can rid their community of those who do not uphold traditional values. For information on candidates, see your local Concerned Women for America chapter leader or get in touch with your Christian Coalition leader.

Responsible Christian citizenship in a republic like America needs the participation of all morally concerned citizens in order to survive. Make sure your public leaders share your family values. That way they can provide your community with a family-friendly government. One of the greatest presidents of our lifetime said:

The family has always been the cornerstone of American society. Our families nurture, preserve and pass on to each succeeding generation the values we share and cherish, values that are the foundation for our freedoms. In the family, we learn our first lessons of God and man, love and discipline, rights and responsibilities, human dignity and human frailty.

Today more than ever, it is essential that these contributions not be taken for granted and that each of us remember that the strength of our families is vital to the strength of our nation.

—President Ronald Reagan

Teach Your Children the Work Ethic

It is important that children learn early "there is no free lunch." Someone has to pay for everything. By showering their children with too much, well-meaning parents often teach them that anything they want can be had without effort. That is the hallmark of a too-affluent society. Children need the responsibilities of chores and cooperation around the house in order to get an allowance. They need to learn early the joy of earning the money to buy something they need or want. That way they will treasure it more.

We stress "early" because we have a friend who has worked for 20 years with inner-city youth. In addition to helping them spiritually, he has tried to help them find work by getting Christian businessmen to farm out some of their manufacturing jobs to the inner city. He told us he has to get the kids started working at around 15 years of age when they have a natural instinct to work and earn. Then he said, "If you wait until they are 19 before they get their first job, it is almost impossible to teach them the work ethic." Then he added the amazing comment, "Even when we get a 19 to 20-year-old genuinely converted, if he has never had a job, it is like pulling teeth to teach him the work ethic." No wonder so many inner-city government projects fail.

Government handouts during the past 30 years have proven to be a tragedy because they do not include the biblical mandates that man should earn his bread by the sweat of his face (Genesis 3:19) and "If anyone will not work, neither shall he eat" (2 Thessalonians 3:10). The place to learn the work ethic is in the home—early.

Watch Their Peer Groups

One of the biggest mistakes Christian parents make is to let their teenagers select their own friends. We are all influenced by our friends for good or for bad, depending on the friend. And teenage peer pressure is probably the greatest pressure our children will ever face. That is why if jeans are "in," they all wear jeans. The same is true of long hair, T-shirts, and so on. If "everyone is doing it," your kids may be persuaded by teen peer pressure to do that which is contrary to your moral values. That is why your young person needs an active church group in which to fellowship and, if possible, a Christian school.

"Evil company corrupts good habits" (1 Corinthians 15:33), the verse of Scripture which God revealed in a special way to my widowed mother, kept me from destroying myself when I was 17. Recognizing that my boyhood friends of many years did not share my moral values, she gave me the choice of leaving home or breaking off from my friends. In those days, I couldn't run off to a youth-care center, humanistic guidance counselor, or child advocate who thought humanist bureaucrats knew more about child-raising than parents. After learning that no one loved me more than my mother, I returned home and discovered that those kids at the church weren't so bad after all. One of those boyhood friends spent 16 years in a federal prison. My mother knew I didn't need that kind of influence.

A youth pastor with 25 years of experience told us that, in his opinion, "The biggest mistake most dedicated Christian parents make is when their children become teens, they let them pick out their own friends." A heartbroken mother of a 14-year-old came to Bev's office in Washington after appearing at a government hearing to testify how her daughter almost died after a botched abortion. The mother took her daughter to church regularly and did other right things, but admitted, "On Friday nights I let her go to the mall to be with her friends." Needless to say, that mother had no idea who those friends were or what moral values they possessed.

Young people are most inclined to be emotionally combustible between the ages of 14 and 24. Therefore, screen your offspring from the wrong kind of influence during those very impressionable years.

The Church Is the Most Family-Friendly Institution of Our Day

The greatest friend of the family is the church, and that is as our Creator intended. When I say "church," I am assuming a Bible-teaching church that communicates God's principles for family living to its members. One of the best things a couple can do for their children is to find such a church and use it to help them raise their children to love and serve God.

The church is the one place a family can go where the values they are trying to instill in their children at home will be supported and reinforced. We have all heard of "the power of the pulpit." Never underestimate its effectiveness. All parents need that outside voice—the pastor, Sunday school teacher or youth pastor—to reaffirm the biblical teachings the children receive at home. This ring of insulation is so powerful that we will dedicate all of chapter 12 to it.

Your Spiritual Resources

The most powerful ring of insulation against the attacks we have discussed is your spiritual resources. We are taught in the Scriptures that "For we do not wrestle against flesh and blood, but against . . . spiritual hosts of wickedness in the heavenly places" (Ephesians 6:12). To counter these satanic attacks on our lives and homes, we need to utilize all the spiritual resources available to us.

Make Yours a Family-Life University

The home should be the world's greatest university. Mother and Father are universally the most important teachers in the life of a child. Even untrained parents can be effective teachers. God has given parents a special place in the hearts of their children, particularly during their early years, when they can teach them almost anything.

Because young children have extremely curious and impressionable minds, they should be exposed to biblical truth early and regularly by the two most effective teachers in their lives: Mom and Dad. Such instruction will provide excellent insulation against humanism's battle for their minds. The following four teaching methods will provide an excellent curriculum for your family college.

1. *Daily family devotions.* Most churches encourage their families to spend 10 to 30 minutes a day in family worship or daily devotions. This simple but effective family habit

provides many benefits. It not only trains the children to acknowledge and respect God, but also creates in them an early responsiveness to His Word as a book above all others, and that it is valuable to read daily. The father should lead in this short devotional time, establishing it as an important priority throughout life, particularly when the children are in their teen years.

Daily devotions provide an opportunity for parents to teach their children to pray and to discuss principles from the Bible. Your Bible bookstore contains several good books and aids on this subject, if your church does not supply such materials. The following sample outline may prove helpful, but remember to keep family devotions age-appropriate.

> Read the Bible—one chapter or less if the children are small.
> Read a daily devotional guide.
> Briefly discuss what you have read—ask the children simple questions.
> Review a Scripture memory verse.
> Assign subjects for prayer.
> Assign prayer requests.
> Pray—one or two children (depending on family size) and one parent.
> Sing a song of praise to God.

2. *Consistent Christian example.* Children are the world's greatest imitators. Just as angry and selfish children are reared in angry, selfish homes, so loving, joyful, and thankful children come out of Spirit-filled homes because they have seen these characteristics exemplified in the conduct of their parents. Integrity, honesty, industry, and consideration for others are not only taught but "caught" by children as they grow up, if such traits appear on a day-to-day basis in the lives of their parents. The power of a good example to overcome the harmful forces working to destroy our youth cannot be overestimated.

In the youth ministry of our church, from which hundreds of young people have entered the ministry or some form of Christian work as a life vocation, the pastoral staff has noted that such young people usually come from two kinds of families: Spirit-filled homes of consistency or families in which one or both parents are not Christians. Rarely do they come from carnal Christian homes. Young people can understand their parents' unchristian behavior if they are not believers, so it doesn't always have an adverse effect upon them. But they cannot cope with inconsistent carnality from those who should be walking in the Spirit. The greatest blessing any parent can give his child is a consistent example in the home. Its powerful impact can extend even to the third and fourth generation (Exodus 20:5).

3. *Loving discipline.* The worst experience for any child is to regularly get his own way. But almost every child tries: Human nature insists on it. That is why he must learn in the home to control his desires by self-denial or parental denial. If he does not receive that loving discipline from his parents, he will grow up to be a self-guided missile waiting for disaster.

For 35 years a form of permissiveness that grew out of humanistic psychology has been popular in our country, and as a result three generations of self-indulgent people have become very hostile if they cannot assert their wants or "rights." The exception to that general rule of thumb are those who were blessed with parents cognizant of the biblical principle, "He who spares his rod hates his son" (Proverbs 13:24).

As a veteran father, I will admit that disciplining my children was the most difficult aspect of fatherhood, but it was essential. In fact, not until my son had to spank his own son did he really understand that it had hurt me worse than it did him. The necessity of that kind of discipline is not only confirmed in the Bible many times (Proverbs 13:24; 23:13,14; 29:15) but is also validated in life. Susanna Wesley, the successful mother of 17 children, said, "The child that does not learn to obey his parents in the home will not obey God or man out of the home." Children need instruction, but they also require correction, particularly when they demonstrate rebellion.

Dr. James Dobson, the child psychologist whose bestselling books on parental instruction are among the finest in print, teaches that parents should carefully distinguish between the mistakes a child makes and the rebellion he expresses. For example, I have heard him say, "Never spank a child for mistakes, but always spank him for rebellion." The Bible teaches, "Rebellion is as the sin of witchcraft" (1 Samuel 15:23).

One word of caution on discipline is in order. Never spank your children when you are angry. That is when parents abuse their children. Anger not only grieves the Spirit, but it also renders a person so out of control emotionally that they can do things under its influence they regret the rest of their lives. For that reason, always wait until you calm down so that you can "apply the rod of learning to the seat of understanding" without inflicting lasting damage. Then, within ten minutes or less, go back and reassure the child of your love. All discipline should convey clearly that it is the act of disobedience you disapprove of, not the child. And one other thing. When the discipline is over, don't bring it up again. We need to be like our heavenly Father, who, after we have confessed our sins, remembers them against us no more.

4. *A personal salvation experience for each member of the family.* God has so planned that every person shall give an account of himself to his heavenly Father, which explains why it is essential for children to have their own conversion experiences. If we, as parents, could invite Christ into our children's hearts by faith, doubtless we would. But that is an experience the child must gain for himself when he reaches that age at which he understands with his head, believes in his heart, and surrenders his will to the call of Christ.

For most children who are raised in a Christian home and attend a Bible-teaching church, that experience occurs at a very early age. In the case of our first child, who was very responsive to spiritual things, she understood basic biblical truth sufficiently to invite Christ into her heart at four years of age. Now she is married to a minister, and all three of her children have received the Savior at nearly the same early age. Others of our children waited until six or seven. Parents should be sensitive to the spiritual yearnings of each child. Do not pressure very young children, lest their desire be to please you rather than to surrender their own wills to Jesus Christ. On the other hand, older children should be an increasing object of prayerful concern by their parents if they have not received Christ before their twelfth birthday.

Wise parents will occasionally give opportunity for their young children to rehearse their conversion experiences in order to keep them fresh and personal in their minds, either by reminding them of the details or by helping them to verbalize them. In addition, the Bible says, "Let the redeemed of the LORD say so" (Psalm 107:2). Children need to hear occasionally how their parents came to Christ and the events surrounding the conversion of their brothers and sisters.

The individual conversion has been mentioned first because it is the most basic spiritual experience. If parents take this step for granted, the children may enter the precarious stage of puberty and youth without it. Young people frequently turn away from the Lord, His church, and their parents when confronted with drugs, rock music, and humanism in school because they lack this foundational spiritual experience to insulate them from temptations.

Your Family's Personal Insulation

Your family is your most important possession. Until the ravages of our humanistic culture are removed, you must carefully protect them as if your life depends on it, for theirs does. It is still possible to raise a family to love and serve God today, but as we've said, it takes more effort and time than it ever has. Make your family your most important priority, and with God's help, you and your loved ones can make it. Many people have confessed to me, "If I had my life to live over, I would spend more time with my family." I have never had one say, "If I had my life to live over, I would spend less time with my family." Nor have I heard a businessman say, "If I had my life to live over, I would spend more time at the office." Some of our books based on the above messages that will help you are:

The Battle for the Mind

The Battle for the Family

A Nation Without a Conscience

Spirit-Controlled Temperament

I Love You, But Why Are We So Different?

The Act of Marriage

How to Be Happy Though Married

Against the Tide: How to Raise Sexually Pure Kids in an "Anything-Goes" World

It is still possible to insulate your family from the evil effects of our hostile culture, with God's help and a good church.

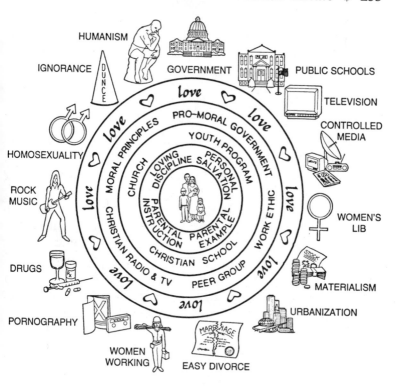

MEMO
To: Parents
From: A Child

1. Don't spoil me. I know quite well that I ought not to have all I ask for—I'm only testing you.
2. Don't be afraid to be firm with me. I prefer it; it makes me feel secure.
3. Don't let me form bad habits. I have to rely on you to detect them in the early stages.
4. Don't make me feel smaller than I am. It only makes me behave stupidly "big."
5. Don't correct me in front of people if you can help it. I'll take much more notice if you talk quietly with me in private.

6. Don't make me feel that my mistakes are sins. It upsets my sense of values.

7. Don't protect me from consequences. I need to learn the painful way sometimes.

8. Don't be too upset when I say "I hate you." Sometimes it isn't you I hate but your power to thwart me.

9. Don't take too much notice of my small ailments. Sometimes they get me the attention I need.

10. Don't nag. If you do, I shall have to protect myself by appearing deaf.

11. Don't forget that I cannot explain myself as well as I should like. That is why I am not always accurate.

12. Don't put me off when I ask questions. If you do, you will find that I stop asking and seek my information else where.

13. Don't be inconsistent. That completely confuses me and makes me lose faith in you.

14. Don't tell me my fears are silly. They are terribly real and you can do much to reassure me if you try to understand.

15. Don't ever suggest that you are perfect or infallible. It gives me too great a shock when I discover that you are neither.

16. Don't ever think that it is beneath your dignity to apologize to me. An honest apology makes me feel surprisingly warm towards you.

17. Don't forget I love experimenting. I couldn't get along without it, so please put up with it.

18. Don't forget how quickly I am growing up. It must be very difficult for you to keep pace with me, but please do try.

19. Don't forget that I don't thrive without lots of love and understanding, but I don't need to tell you, do I?

20. Please keep yourself fit and healthy. I need you.

—Source unknown

Chapter 12

The Church and Your Family

$\mathcal{O}$n a scale of 1 to 8, where your family decides to go to church will rank about number 5 in life's most important decisions. The top four decisions cover accepting Christ as Lord and Savior, deciding on a vocation, selecting a partner, and choosing a place to live. Unfortunately, most Christians do not realize the great influence of the church on their families.

Active participation in a Bible-teaching church will provide many safeguards against the erosion of family life. The church is the best agency for training people in the principles of happy family living. Consequently, the church enjoys a much lower divorce level than that of the secular community. Of the 890 active families that were in our church, which was probably typical of Bible-teaching churches for Southern California, there were 40 which had been struck by divorce. In other words, one out of 22 of our church families experienced divorce, compared to one out of two in the community in general.

This means that Christian marriages in our area were 11 times as stable as nonchurch unions. If the divorce rate is lowered 11 times, we can assume that the happiness quotient is increased equally. (Southern California churches may have a higher rate of divorce than Christians nationally, because many divorced believers move west after undergoing such a trauma, thus inflating these numbers.) However, the divorce rate has also increased alarmingly in churches throughout America because many Christians imitate the world and its ways, rather than obediently following the principles of God.

A couple who visited our Sunday-morning service introduced themselves and said, "Before buying a lot and building a house, we wanted to be sure there was a good church in this community." I wish more Christians demonstrated such foresight. Most folks who built in that area probably had no idea what kind of church was available. Since ours was the only one for several miles, it could have been tragic for them and their children if we had not preached the gospel. Some Christians do not understand that the church they attend can be a dynamic influence on their entire family. It can help them mature spiritually, enrich their marriage relationship, and enable their children to face life's adjustments. Or it can freeze them spiritually and seriously jeopardize every area of their lives. A Bible-teaching church with a life-related message can make it considerably easier for parents to discharge their responsibilities to raise their children in the "fear and admonition of the Lord."

Wherever the gospel has been preached, churches have sprung up. In New Testament times it was customary for Christians to meet in homes or halls on a regular basis for the study of the Bible, fellowship with one another, and the "breaking of bread." Such meetings helped new Christians to grow in the faith, to face persecution, and to go out and share their faith in the power of the Holy Spirit.

Through 19 centuries of history, bodies of believers have regularly joined together. These assemblies, or churches, have been the instruments by which God has kept His message alive and presented it to the world. Satan has consistently tried to destroy them through persecution, heresy, division, apostasy, friction, worldly conformity, and a host of other vicious or subtle attacks.

In the course of the centuries, God has raised up certain groups and organizations which have been used mightily in such specialized areas as youth, missions, education, and so on. Some of them have hit a peak in effectiveness and then faded away. The one tool God has used through the centuries and is still using today is His church.

The last book of the Bible describes seven local churches as "lampstands" (or lighthouses) of the gospel (Revelation 1-3). It pictures Christ walking among the lampstands (or churches), willing to empower, enlighten, and provide for any church that wants to do His will. This great book of prophecy indicates that our Lord ordained the continuing ministry of the local church. In the Gospel of Matthew, He said of the church, "The gates of Hades shall not prevail against it" (Matthew 16:18). The church is the only permanent institution the family can still rely on.

Today the local church is one of the few places where the spiritual life of an individual can be nurtured. As we have seen, television, radio, magazines, newspapers, all other news media, and the public schools are practically devoid of any contribution to spiritual edification. Instead, they propagate philosophies that are worldly and quite contrary to the Word of God.

There was a time when the principles of the Bible were applied to most aspects of life. Our economy was based on integrity and hard work. Many laws were based on scriptural teaching. Every man was responsible for himself, but biblical concern for one's neighbor was a way of life. Christian principles were not always practiced, but basically they were the accepted standards. Our schools recognized the existence of God and used the Bible freely in the classroom.

Today all that has been changed. Parents who want their children to learn the truth about God can expect little or no

238 ✦ The Spirit-Filled Family

help from the schools. The best place to expose them to Christian teaching, next to the home itself, is the church. Through its Bible-teaching services, Sunday school, youth groups, Bible studies, and other activities, the church is equipped to contribute to the spiritual training of the whole family. If a person neglects the church, his family is almost certain to grow up with an entirely secular education and philosophy of life.

The church is probably the most underrated organization in the world today. Admittedly, it is not perfect, but it is the tool created especially by God to reach the world for Christ. The church is indispensable to a Christian and his family.

Purpose of the Church

If it teaches the Bible, a church can fulfill a unique position by offering something vital to every member of a family. The Scriptures were written to help spiritual "children . . . young men . . . [and] fathers" (1 John 2:12-14). When the Bible is properly taught, it provides spiritual food for every person, adapted to his personal needs.

A church also meets the basic need of every human being to serve his fellowman. As we shall see, anyone who sincerely wants to help another may do so in his local church—in teaching, youth work, visitation, or whatever he is qualified to do.

A church also provides opportunities for enjoyable fellowship and making friends on every level. At church, wholesome relationships can be formed. Children, young people, newlyweds, parents, and senior citizens are going to make friends somewhere. Where better than in the church, where they are likely to find people of similar interests and standards?

How to Choose a Church

Since your church can have such a profound effect on your life, the selection of a church is vitally important. You should not just attend the nearest church. The first consideration is usually the denomination, but the final decision should be based on the message preached and the opportunity for biblical worship and service, as well as on the total potential impact on the entire family. The following suggestions will be helpful in choosing a family church:

1. *Pray for wisdom.* God promises wisdom (James 1:5) for those who seek His counsel in making decisions. The entire family should join in this prayer, for the chosen church will be everyone's spiritual home. Good human judgment is important, but only God knows what a church will be 2, 5, or 20 years from now.

2. *Loyalty to the Bible is a primary characteristic of a good church.* As you visit various churches, evaluate them in the light of how much balanced and careful exposure to the Word of God your family will receive there. Examine the Sunday school literature for Bible content. No amount of enthusiasm, promotion, or organization can replace solid Bible teaching.

Church services vary, depending on the denomination and the area of the country. Your tastes and preferences are more than likely based on your background and temperament. Churches, like people, have personalities. It is important to feel comfortable in your home church, but comfort or enjoyment of form is not as important as Bible teaching. It is possible to go sound asleep in a "comfortable" church and, before you realize it, start drifting spiritually.

My uncle, Dr. Elmer Palmer, was a pastor for 53 years. When I was 25 and just starting out in the ministry, he advised me, "Feed the people big hunks of beefsteak from the Word of God every time you preach." As a result, I have always given my sermons "the beefsteak test." That is, do they contain a great deal of Bible and a little of Tim LaHaye? That kind of preaching builds strong spiritual members, so look for that type of church for your family.

3. *Your church should minister to your entire family.* Some churches are strong in youth work, some in the area of children, and some provide a fine program for adults. Visit the youth meetings, Sunday school, or training-hour departments which members of your family will attend, so you will know firsthand what is being taught and who is teaching it. If you want your children and young people to remain open to the leading of the Holy Spirit for a lifetime of Christian service, examine your prospective church to see how many of its former youth are in or are preparing for Christian work. It is estimated that over 85 percent of today's pastors and missionaries responded to God's call to service in Sunday school, church, or youth camp.

Many good churches are catching the vision of starting Christian schools. The deterioration of the public schools morally, spiritually, philosophically, and (according to recently published test scores) educationally, causes Christian parents to look to their church for the proper education of their children. In an increasing number of public schools, the incidence of violence, rape, and drug abuse renders them totally unacceptable to the Christian community. Personally, I am convinced, after many years of involvement in Christian-school education, that it is the wave of the future.

Lest you think I am exaggerating, let me tell you this story. While being evaluated for accreditation (which we subsequently received) by the Western Association of Schools and Colleges, our high school was visited by a team of five educators. One was a Christian who quickly identified himself. Three were principals of enormous public high schools in their respective communities. Two of them confidentially shared with me that they sent their daughters to *Christian* schools in their community. A week or so later I attended a social activity and met the president of the San Diego Unified School Board, who told me his daughter attended our Christian high school and loved it.

4. *Your church should provide you a place to serve God.* Admittedly, there may be other areas of Christian service in your community, but usually a Christian can work most effectively in his own church. Most churches require that you be a member before you teach or hold an office. The pastor, Christian-education director, or Sunday school superintendent will tell you how your prospective church can use your services.

5. *Your church should be one you can confidently recommend to others.* Every Christian should anticipate that God will use him as a witness at his work, in his neighborhood, or in his other contacts. It is not enough for you to lead people to Christ. Your new converts will need Christian fellowship and Bible instruction in a warmly spiritual environment. It is easier to get them to meet you at your church than to send them to another church alone.

Get the Most from Your Church

Once you have settled on the church you feel God is leading you to, join it. Make it your family's spiritual home. One of the oldest clichés reminds us, "You get out of a thing only what you put into it." Some Christians sow so little seed that they harvest next to nothing.

Most churches expect their members to assume some responsibilities as much for the members' good as for the benefit of the church. You and your family will receive rich blessings when you faithfully fulfill such responsibilities.

Every church has a few members who attend every service; they usually reap the greatest dividends. Others attend both Sunday morning and evening but never come to weeknight services. The majority gain minimum blessing from their church because they attend only on Sunday morning. The more secular our society becomes, the more believers need to expose themselves to the Word of God—an experience which most Christians enjoy only at the services of their churches.

There are 168 hours in a week. Obviously, one or two hours spent in the Lord's house, studying His Word, is meager compared to the time devoted to life's other activities. Though the Word of God is the most important subject of study for a Christian, most believers do not give it as much time as they devote to the daily newspaper.

One common hindrance to regular family church attendance is the notion that we may embitter teenagers by forcing them to go to church. On a number of occasions through the years, I have heard overindulgent parents say, "I don't make my child go to church. He might grow up to hate it."

One Christian couple told their son that if he didn't want to attend church, he could go to the local drugstore and get a malt while waiting for his parents. Somehow my sermons never seemed to compete with that lad's love for malts, and today, married and the father of three, he still does not attend church.

In that same church was a family with five sons. Their father made the decision for them: Every Sunday they went to church. They sat with their parents during morning worship but were permitted to sit with friends at other services, if their conduct warranted such liberty. Today one boy is on the mission field and the others are active leaders in local churches.

Don't be afraid of making the decision for your young people about attending church. You don't hesitate to send them to school, whether they want to go or not. And how often do your children *want* to visit the dentist or the doctor? But you make them go if they *need* to. Your children desperately need the church and the consistent opportunity it gives them to worship and to learn God's will. I thank God for my mother who, when I was a rebellious 17-year-old, made it clear that I was to be at practically every service our church held. I doubt that I would be in the ministry today if I had been left to make my own decisions about church attendance during those years.

Forcing a child to attend services doesn't turn him against the church. It is often hypocrisy in the home that does that. Young people expect their parents to live in the home what they learn in church. I have seen few children from consistent Christian homes go down the drain. Among the few who have, most come back to their faith later in life (see Proverbs 22:6).

One of the duties most lightly esteemed by many church members is attendance at business meetings. This may sound insignificant, but you would be amazed how few people care enough about the operation of their own church to participate in its business. Several pastor friends have told me they can hardly muster enough people for a quorum. I would be the first to admit that church business meetings are not the most inspirational sessions to attend, but their importance to the church requires that they be given priority.

For any organization to function, it must have leaders. The only way to limit the number of business meetings a church must hold is to have leaders who can operate the church effectively. Your church has a right to expect you to devote some of your time to its business.

There are other areas in which your church needs you, and the Lord will lead you into them if you are available. One of the finest church laymen I know is an executive in a large industrial manufacturing company. Each year he looks over his church to discover areas of greatest need. He makes himself available to the Lord, his pastor, and the officers in the church by volunteering for that area of service. If he is given a job, he dedicates himself to performing well and tries to train another layman to replace him in the future. Sometimes the church isn't ready to delegate the job to his trainee after the first year, so he stays on one year more. Only God knows the full effectiveness of this man's ministry through the years.

No church is perfect! The late Dr. Harry A. Ironside used to say, "If you find the perfect church, don't join it; you'll ruin it!" You are bound to find things wrong with your church. But *never* criticize it, the pastor, the leaders, or the members in front of your children. Many thoughtless words of parental criticism against some detail have turned children against the whole church. Parents, not the church, are the real losers in a case like this, but so are their children. Instead of criticizing your church, put your shoulder to the wheel and *change* it. And if the wrong is not in an area of your responsibility, commit it to God. After all, it's really *His* church; He is well able to take care of it.

Social Life and Your Church

God has made most of us with a craving for social life. We want to be loved, sought out, and included in whatever is going on. The church has the potential of being one of the finest sources of social contact, but unfortunately, the selfish and impersonal attitude of the world is too often carried over into the social life of the church.

Many people are lonely and hungry for fellowship. They visit your church hoping to make friends, but often those to whom they look for friendship do nothing to meet their need. Have you ever opened your home to such people? Many church members never do. They are busy enjoying the friends they already have. It takes a little work, and you may have to bake some cookies and put on a pot of coffee, but you'll be amazed how rewarding it is!

Have you ever thought about the social vacuum many new converts are plunged into when they join a church? If they were active social types before their conversion, they are often in for a discouraging experience when they lose interest in some of their worldly activities and look to the church. Too frequently, it is difficult or impossible for these strangers to break into the cliques that have established themselves in a church. We don't like to admit it, but cliques develop all too easily when we naturally gravitate to our friends. Remember that new or prospective Christians need your love and attention far more than your old friends do!

Several years ago, three couples in our church hit on a novel idea. They decided to share in providing dinner in one of their homes for themselves and three other couples once a month. They would invite one regular-member family and two new couples. Within two years, they had more friends in the church than anyone else. Their own spiritual growth has been amazing, and today one of these couples serves as missionaries in Ecuador, another joined the staff of Campus Crusade, and the third is counted among the pillars of our church.

One Spirit-filled woman I know decided to volunteer as the social chairman of an adult Sunday school class. The Bible teaching was good on Sunday, but the class members were impersonal and aloof toward each other. She soon had things jumping by careful planning and by involving many others who were waiting for someone to invite them to climb down out of the grandstand. Instead of one big social a month, she would often arrange to have eight or ten small groups meeting in various parts of the city. Sometimes she would ask people in a certain geographical area to serve a snack after church and to invite class visitors. Her service as a Sunday-school-class chairman had real impact on the whole Sunday school's attendance. Sporadic visitors to Sunday school became regular in their attendance, some invited their unsaved friends, and a number received Christ during this woman's two years of service.

Since adults were attending more regularly and bringing their children and young people, the entire Sunday school experienced its largest growth rate in our church's history, and that woman was probably the most important single reason. Lifetime friendships were made in that adult class, and many of them were hers.

Hospitality with a Purpose

Christians should be "given to hospitality." Never have more Christians had nicer homes in which to be hospitable, yet somehow other pursuits too often take priority over entertaining those who need our hospitality.

A young dentist called one day and asked if we would come over on a Sunday evening after church to help him and his wife dedicate their new home. It was packed with church friends when we arrived, and we enjoyed a warm time of singing, prayer, and fellowship. They told the group they wanted God to use their home for His glory, and during the next few years hundreds of people were their guests. Only God knows how many have been drawn to Him by this generous Christian hospitality.

Many Christians in all parts of the country are using their homes in hospitality evangelism. Some have informal Bible studies and refreshments; others have tapes or speakers. Their experience shows that many people are hungry for the Word of God. Home Bible studies provide a neutral place for new converts to bring unsaved friends to study the Word. At first these "prospects" may not be willing to go to a church, but usually they aren't reluctant to attend a Bible study in a hospitable Christian home.

One couple has led more people to Christ and into our church than any other that I know of, and they have used their home to do it. About three years after their conversion, they started to entertain their unsaved friends and some of their new Christian friends from the church. One night they stumbled on the idea of playing a taped sermon and then discussing it over coffee and dessert. Now the couple listens to the tape in advance, thinks up questions to spark discussion, and then invites 20 or 30 people, aiming at a balance of one unsaved person to two Christians. Since neither of them has had any formal Bible training, they try to make sure there are two or three mature believers among their guests.

Through the years I have seen these folks lead doctors, dentists, lawyers, plumbers, mechanics, and housewives to faith in Christ. One refreshing aspect of their work is that they do not concentrate on the "up-and-outer." To them the couple with the rickety old car is as important as the owner of the luxury sedan. After watching them, I am convinced that their ministry could be duplicated by any Christian willing to make his home available to God.

"Hospitality with a purpose" is a form of Christian service that has its origin in the church, is based in the home, and is pointed toward reaching people. Christians often think their home is not good enough in which to entertain, but other people aren't primarily interested in your furnishings or in the refreshments you serve. They will love you for including them as your guests. That's why this kind of ministry can be so effective, because of the need for love and acceptance. More people are won to Christ through love than through logic.

If you are interested in using your home for "hospitality with a purpose," offer it to God in prayer and start experimenting with some of these suggestions or others the Lord may give you. It won't be long before you'll feel comfortable in a ministry of hospitality.

How Best to Serve

The church is one of the best employment opportunities in the world, for it is a place where everyone may, and should, serve. Any dedicated Christian who wants to be used by God can find something to do in the Sunday school, the nursery, the youth programs, or driving a bus, visiting, having home Bible classes, and so on.

There is tremendous therapy in Christian service. Every human being needs to invest himself in something for the good of his fellowman. Nothing equals the significance of Christian service, for through it you not only help a person live a better life but also enable him to face eternity.

Practically everyone today is concerned about the problems faced by young people: rebellion, dope, sex, and many other areas. But few people are willing to do much about the situation. The same is true in the church. Everyone wants a dynamic youth ministry, but it is harder to attract youth sponsors for such a ministry than it is to get almost any other workers in the church. People have the false notion that one must possess special talent or training to work with young people. Really, today's young people aren't that "different." The primary requirement for a Christian who is to work with children or youth is to have a love for them. Even the hardest cases respond to patient, tactful Christian love.

The best way to learn how to work with young people is by doing it. Good books, seminars, and clinics are available to help you master techniques, but experience and necessity are still excellent teachers. We have found that parents with young people of their own in a given department make great helpers in a youth group for that age. Their children, rather than feeling uncomfortable in such a setup, are usually pleased to have their parents that involved.

Most young people, sooner or later, go through an uncooperative phase and decide, "I'm not going." If the parent gives in, he is making a big mistake. If young people don't attend youth meetings and socials, they soon drift out into the world and make friends who take them away from the church. It seems better to insist, if necessary, that your teens go to youth activities and take their unsaved friends with them from time to time. Many a Christian today was an unsaved teenager whose buddy took him to church youth functions.

By our own example, we need to teach our children and youth to have a concern for other people. Someone has likened a church to a gigantic sieve. Hundreds of hungry souls come looking for help but get so little attention that they slip right through our ranks without leaving a trace. If young people see their parents going out of their way to befriend newcomers at church, it is easy to get them to do the same in their youth groups, where love and acceptance are also often sadly lacking.

Space does not permit mention of all the other much-needed areas that provide us a place to serve the Lord in the church. Of one thing you can be certain: If you offer your talents to God, He will lead you to a meaningful ministry. Don't overlook the nursery, choir, or groups such as Pioneer Girls and Boys' Brigade. If you can't sing, be a "choir mother" for a children's or youth choir. Men can do repair and maintenance work on buildings and yard work on the grounds. Visitation, being a home group leader, and Sunday-school teaching are other options.

We hear a lot today about "involvement," and that is exactly what Christians should have in their churches. In such involvement they not only help others, but also are participating in the greatest work in the world.

Some time ago, a couple from our former church in Minneapolis dropped by for a visit. We talked of the day, 25 years before, when the Sunday school superintendent and I had asked Bob, the husband, to teach a junior-department class of boys. We both laughed when I reminded him that after one year of teaching he candidly told me, "Pastor, I have learned more from teaching that class than I ever did listening to your sermons." Admitting that he was still teaching a class after all these years, he said, "Next to rearing my family, teaching is the most rewarding thing I do." That man had the idea, and I couldn't help adding that teaching is one thing he does that will have eternal results. The church provides many jobs like that for Spirit-filled Christians. What are you doing in *your* church?

Chapter 13

Prayer Power
for Family Living

*T*he only problem in reading a book like this is that it exposes our weaknesses or failings and tends to leave us discouraged. Frequently we hear folks say after our Family Life Seminar, "I wish we had heard these principles years ago!" Our honest answer is, "So do we!" Fortunately, we have some encouraging words for you.

You Don't Have to Be Perfect!

No parent has ever been perfect. We certainly weren't! If Bev and I had our parenting days to live over, you can be sure we would do many things differently. I wish we had discovered the Spirit-filled life before our oldest child was born. We would have been better parents. But even then, we wouldn't have been perfect. I wish we could say that since the thrilling experience at Forest Home, when God began to change our lives, we have been ideal parents. But God and our children know better. There is no question that we are much improved. But perfect? I am sorry to disillusion you. We weren't and still aren't. Fortunately, God doesn't expect perfection, and neither do your children. The Bible teaches, "All have sinned and fall short of the glory of God" (Romans 3:23). That includes even Christian parents. Because Spirit-filled Christians are not robots, we still give in to our old sin nature and react in the flesh on occasion. Hopefully, after studying this book, you have gained the realization that if you will quickly face and confess your sin you will be immediately restored and *gradually* begin to "walk in the Spirit" on a regular basis. As you develop a keen sensitivity to sin, your times of carnality will become less frequent and love, joy, peace, longsuffering, and goodness will become a way of life.

The Christian Court of Last Appeals

A weeping wife and mother stopped me after a seminar and sobbed, "Is there any hope for a parent who has done everything wrong?"

"Of course!" I replied. Why? Because we Christians have a resource that is unshared by any other group of people. What is that extra resource? *The power of prayer.* You are doubtless familiar with the many challenges to prayer our Lord gave in the Gospels: "Ask, and it will be given to you; seek, and you will find. . . . For everyone who asks receives" (Matthew 7:7,8); "Whatever you ask in prayer, believing, you will receive" (Matthew 21:22); "Ask, and you will receive, that your joy may be full" (John 16:24); "Men always ought to pray and not lose heart" (Luke 18:1); and many others. The Old Testament tells us, "The prayer of the upright is His [God's] delight" (Proverbs 15:8).

In the Epistles of the New Testament, we find scores of challenges to prayer: "Pray without ceasing" (1 Thessalonians 5:17); "In everything by prayer and supplication, with thanksgiving, let your requests be made known to God" (Philippians 4:6); "The effective, fervent prayer of a righteous man avails much" (James 5:16). As Christians we are privileged to address the supreme, omnipotent Creator of all things as "Dear Heavenly Father," for we have been adopted into the family of God. He has made us His children. Our Lord reassured us of God's interest in our prayers when He said, "If you then, being evil, know how to give good gifts to your children, how much more will your Father who is in heaven give good things to those who ask Him!" (Matthew 7:11).

All dedicated parents utilize this prayer power on behalf of their children at some time in their lives, particularly at times of great crisis. Bev and I vividly recall standing at Lori's bedside when at the age of five she had her second bout with pneumonia. Her little chest was heaving as she gasped for every breath under the oxygen tent. Then the doctor said, "Preacher, if you've ever prayed in your life, you had better do it now. I've done all I can do. It is entirely up to God." Bev wept as I prayed, and God gave us a supernatural peace that Lori would get well. In a matter of minutes she passed the crisis, and gradually the power of God restored her health. Almost all families face crises like this at some time during the growing-up years of their children. One of the many pluses of the Christian life is that we have Someone real to turn to at such times. Frankly, I don't know how non-Christians make it.

Prayer is to a family what a roof is to a house; it protects those within from the enemies and adversities of life. In many cases, it even protects the family members from themselves, like the Christian wife who confided that while praying one morning she sensed that her husband had been unfaithful. He had so carefully shielded himself from detection that she didn't have one clue of what he was doing, but she confidently faced him with his sin. He was so flabbergasted that he blurted out, "How did you know?" Her early detection and confrontation resulted in his repentance, and they have enjoyed years of happiness as a result.

Most of us in the ministry today are the result of someone else's prayers, and usually it is our parents'. In my own case it was the prayers of my mother. Sensing that I had returned from the service extremely carnal and rebellious, she became prayerfully concerned. While attending a Bible conference, she talked with Dr. Bob Jones, Sr., after his message one evening, and he prayed for her son Tim. A few weeks later, I came home to her apartment at 2:30 A.M. and found my mother kneeling at the couch, sound asleep. The living room was so small I literally had to step across the back of her legs to get to my bedroom. At first it made me mad and I thought, "It serves her right; I'll leave her there!" But after getting into bed, I couldn't sleep. I knew she had to get up for work at 5:30 A.M., and that she was praying for me when she fell off to sleep. Finally I awakened her, and she went to bed. That scene haunted me for days until I finally dropped my application to a prelaw school and went to Bob Jones University where my life was transformed. I wish every young man had that kind of a praying mother. Prayer won't make up for a lifetime of parental mistakes, but as a pastor I have witnessed life-changing miracles when burdened parents have sought God's power in the lives of their children.

Recently, I encouraged another Christian worker, deeply concerned over two rebellious teenagers, that through prayer these parents, too, had a court of last appeals. Sometimes our kids get so tired of hearing our sermons that they seem to become hardened to the things of the Lord. Into each of our children's lives He brought some other servant of God at just the right time. Bev and I are deeply in debt to such men as our good friend Ken Poure, well-known youth and family-life speaker here in California; Pastor Jim Cook of San Jose; Bill Gothard; Pastor John McArthur; and our children's former youth pastor, Jerry Riffe, plus several others. These men, in response to our prayers, were tools of the Holy Spirit to help our young people sort out their thinking and recommit themselves to God at strategic times in their lives. The Bible says, "Foolishness [rebellion, which is as the sin of witchcraft] is bound up in the heart of a child, but the rod of correction will drive it far from him" (Proverbs 22:15). In this age in which we live, the spirit of rebellion seems to be protracted. What is a parent to do, even when he has made some mistakes? Prayer is the answer! Spirit-controlled parents have power in prayer.

One of our children fell in love with another Christian (we never permitted them to date non-Christians) who was not really controlled by the Spirit. After praying about their relationship, I became deeply burdened that it shouldn't last, so I told Bev. Her eyes filled with tears and she said, "The Lord has given me the same burden." After praying together about it, we had a talk with our teen. I won't kid you; the response was not pleasant! But we shared our concern in love, and a few months later they lost interest in each other. God has not given us these children to raise by ourselves, but has left us the Bible—the best manual on child raising and interpersonal relationships ever written—and the power of prayer to help our children on their way, particularly at difficult times.

When Sam Lost his Bible

The most beautiful story along this line I have ever heard was shared by a young architect in our church about his youngest brother, Sam. It seems that Sam lost his Bible in the Northwest woods while on a vacation with his parents. Another Christian family rented the cabin some time later and found the Bible, but no name or address inside. They did find this inscription on the first page: "To our son with love, Mom and Dad." The couple was so impressed with this young man by reading the notes he had carefully written throughout his Bible that they called it to the attention of their children. That night at devotions, the father prayed for this lad and then for his own teenage daughter, that someday the Lord would bring into her life a godly young man like the one who had owned the Bible.

Years passed and they all forgot the experience. Eventually their daughter grew up and fell in love with a fine young man she met in a college-age youth camp, and they became engaged. One month before their wedding, the girl's parents were moving, and her fiancé came over to help them. As he picked up a box of books in the study, he saw an old Bible on the top. Setting the box down quickly, he examined it and exclaimed, "Where did you find my Bible?" Everyone was incredulous! Pointing to the inscription inside, he said, "See, it was given to me by my parents." Then, turning to the cover, he showed them the faded gold letters of his name, "Samuel," but his last name had been worn off. It seems that these two Christian families, who lived over a hundred miles apart and did not know each other, had rented the same cabin that summer, one week apart.

Incredible? Impossible? With man, *yes*—with God, *anything is possible!*

Bev and I have no trouble believing that story, and neither did her mother, Mrs. Nell Ratcliffe. The Ratcliffe family joined the First Baptist Church of Farmington, Michigan, shortly after a young widow with three small children had moved to Detroit to live with relatives. Mrs. Ratcliffe remembers the church women praying for "Margaret," the young widow. Because she had been widowed herself when Beverly was only 18 months old, she was moved to pray for this unknown woman that God would supernaturally supply her many needs and enable her to raise her children to serve the Lord. Years passed; Bev and I met in college and were married. Several years later, we were discussing backgrounds, and I happened to mention that our family had received Jesus Christ in the First Baptist Church of Farmington. We discovered that Bev's family had moved there two months after we left for Detroit. Would you believe my widowed mother's first name is *Margaret?*

Yes, God answers prayer. He loves you and wants you to use prayer as a tool of blessing for every member of your family.

> Call to Me, and I will answer you, and show you great and mighty things, which you do not know (Jeremiah 33:3).

*Also by the LaHaye*s

HOW TO DEVELOP YOUR
CHILD'S TEMPERAMENT
by *Beverly LaHaye*

Proven concepts which will help you relate to your children on a one-to-one basis and train each child according to his or her unique temperament. Answers some of the frustrating problems parents face.

HOW TO STUDY THE BIBLE
FOR YOURSELF
by *Tim LaHaye*

This excellent book provides fascinating study helps and charts that will make personal Bible study more interesting and exciting. A three-year program is outlined for a good working knowledge of the Bible.

HOW TO STUDY BIBLE PROPHECY
FOR YOURSELF
by *Tim LaHaye*

Similar in concept and design to *How to Study the Bible for Yourself*, this book guides you through prophetic passages and provides biblical parameters within which to reach your own conclusions about last days' events.

I LOVE YOU, BUT WHY ARE
WE SO DIFFERENT?
by *Tim LaHaye*

Help in understanding *why* opposites attract and how opposite temperaments can enrich both partners, resulting in an incredibly dynamic relationship. Includes biblical principles that will send marriages soaring to new heights.

THE SPIRIT-CONTROLLED WOMAN
by *Beverly LaHaye*

This bestseller gives the Christian woman practical help in understanding herself and the weaknesses she encounters in her private life and in her relationships. Covers every stage of a woman's life.

LaHaye
Temperament
Analysis

- a test to identify your primary and secondary temperaments

- a description of your predominant characteristics

- information regarding your vocational aptitudes and possible vocations suited to you

- recommendations on improving your work habits

- a list of your spiritual gifts in order of their priority

- suggestions for where you can best serve in your church

- steps for overcoming your ten greatest weaknesses

- counsel on marital adjustment and parental leadership

- special advice to singles, divorced persons, pastors, and the widowed

Your personal 13- to 16-page evaluation letter from Dr. Tim LaHaye will be permanently bound in a handsome vinyl leather portfolio.

... your opportunity
to know yourself
better!

$10.00 Discount Certificate
Off regular price of $29.95.

_____

Name

_____

Address

_____

City State/Zip

Send this discount
certificate and your
check for just $19.95
to:

FLS

Family Life Seminars
370 L'Enfant Promenade, S.W. #801
Washington, D.C. 20024